What Book Re
Black Fatherhood: The Guide to Male Parenting

For those searching for answers and tired of mere discussions of the problem *Black Fatherhood* is a must read. It's a book that draws from real black fathers who are taking on the responsibility of raising children. It is not an esoteric text . . . it speaks to the general public and gives an inspiring message.

Columbian Missourian

This book deals with the importance of a father's involvement with his children and with basic principles of good parenting. This well-written book fills a special need for black fathers and belongs in all libraries serving them.

The Library Journal

Dr. Hutchinson is out to set the record straight on black males.

Philadelphia News

Parents of all colors will find this book a powerful and insightful step-by-step guide . . . . It will inspire and restore your confidence in the family.

The Freer Press, Texas

This is a book which is simple in its approach and remarkable in it message that the stereotype of the black father absent from home is false. The author does not tell concerned black fathers how to be successful, rather he adeptly shows how already-successful black fathers toil at their parental jobs, showing what worked and what didn't work for them.

Here is more than a book for black fathers. Much of it is for white, Asian and American Indian dads as well.

The Press-News, Osage, IA

This is a book about what black fathers are doing right.

Black Enterprise

Black Fatherhood presents information and advice offered by black men to black men.

Essence Magazine

Perhaps the most compelling thing about this book is the motivation for its existence, the author's resolve to help make a difference in the lives of Black fathers and their sons and daughters. Strong emphasis is placed on the importance of African-American men either remaining with the family or continuing to participate should they leave. This book offers a unique approach to a complex problem.

Los Angeles Sentinel

Interviews with fathers of different generations, occupations, incomes and family circumstances that explore the special concerns and problems of Black fathers.

Ebony Magazine

Black Fatherhood is good tonic for those who believe that black men are getting a bad rap.

Atlanta Daily World

Hutchinson shows in his book that the male presence is very strong in many African-American homes.

Dorothy Gilliam, Washington Post

Black Fatherhood describes the unique challenges of being a black dad.

Marc Lacey, Los Angeles Times

What I found most refreshing is to hear black men talk for the first time about their experiences of being a father.

Kenneth H. Bonnell, Players

What makes the book worthwhile is the absence of ranting, ravings and excuses. One could literally grab a cup of coffee and finish reading the work in one afternoon with an enough information to make the book an excellent resource addition to any library.

The Indianapolis Recorder

A refreshingly fair and accurate work, Dr. Hutchinson decisively counters the pervasive emphasis on negative images of Black men—both as men, and as fathers. Written carefully, with much sensitivity and compassion, *Black Fatherhood* strives to, and succeeds at presenting a balanced view of the numbers of African American men who do actively care for their children.

Ebony Man Magazine

Publisher
MIDDLE PASSAGE PRESS
5517 Secrest Drive
Los Angeles, CA 90043-2029
(213) 298-0266

Printed and bound in the United States.

Publisher's Cataloging in Publication
(Prepared by Quality Books Inc.)

Hutchinson, Earl.
    Black fatherhood II : Black women talk about their men /
Earl Ofari Hutchinson.
    p. cm.
    Includes bibliographical references and index.
    ISBN 1-881032-10-8.
    1. Fatherhood—United States. 2. Afro-American men—
Family relationships. 3. Afro-American parents. 4. Fathers
and daughter—United States. 5. Man-woman relationships.
I. Title. II. Title: Black fatherhood two.

HQ756.H8 1994

                                    306.8'742'089960'73
                                    93-080992

Black Fatherhood II
Black Women Talk About Their Men

Earl Ofari Hutchinson, Ph.D.

MIDDLE PASSAGE PRESS
LOS ANGELES, CA

Books by Earl Ofari Hutchinson, Ph.D.

The Myth of Black Capitalism
Let Your Motto Be Resistance
The Mugging of Black America
Black Fatherhood: The Guide to Male Parenting

Acknowledgements

I thank the following people who patiently read this manuscript and provided critical comments: Dr. Gloria Haithman-Ali, Matt Blair, Dorothy Carter, Joye Day, Yvonne Divans, Sikivu Hutchinson, Candace Burton, Stephanie Sharp.

Front cover illustration and design by Jonathan Smith.

*To African-American women who
truly stand by their men.*

Contents

INTRODUCTION

In my previous book, *Black Fatherhood: The Guide to Male Parenting*, I asked: "Ain't I father too?" The "I" referred to black fathers. It may sound like a strange, perhaps even ridiculous question. But it's a question that has to be asked because the popular media image of black men as derelicts, criminals, drug addicts and gang bangers has been encoded in the thinking of many Americans. If black men are seen as grotesque caricatures, rather than productive achievers, it is impossible to believe they can be responsible fathers.

The fathers I interviewed in *Black Fatherhood* eloquently defended their right to be called fathers. They spoke of the joy and the pain of fatherhood. They spoke of their struggles to maintain relationships. They spoke of their experiences in trying to bring their children safely through the gauntlet of American problems. They offered helpful hints for young black men trying to become responsible nurturers and providers for their children.

Most importantly, they spoke of what it meant to be a black man in America. Yet their experiences were universal and could apply to non-black men as well. *Black Fatherhood* was the first real effort by black men to set the record straight about their experiences as fathers.

Still there was something missing. We needed to hear the voices of those who know them better than anyone else, their women. Only black women can complete the portrait. Why? Because, as one very insightful black woman said, "You cannot separate men from women when you're black." What she meant was that black men and women have forged a bond almost exclusively tied by their common racial suffering.

The bond was forged in West Africa. Despite the common conception of West African society as "male-dominated," the talents and skills of women were prized and valued. Whether they belonged to the Ibo, Yoruba, Ashanti, Yako, or Dahomey societies, women traded, produced food and were the custodians of the song, dance and cultural traditions in their societies.

Their roles as child bearers and rearers were not considered dreary chores, but highly esteemed honors. The Ashanti believed that the duties of women were the foundation of all social relations.

Slavery destroyed the traditional relationships in African society and blurred the gender lines between African men and women. They were no longer wives and mothers, husbands and fathers. They were beasts of burden whose sole function was to enhance the profit and power of the slave masters.

> Nobody ever help me into carriages, or ober mud puddles, or gives me any best places. Look at my arms! I have plowed and planted and gathered into barns, and no man could head me—and aren't I a woman?

Sojourner Truth was right. The chains and shackles did not encase black men alone, they encased black women, too. Black men were not the only ones who lay tightly packed on the wooden slats in the holds of slave ships, black women were, too. The millions that were lost in the middle passage were not just black men, but black women, too. The whip and the club of the slave master did not sink deep into the skin of black men only, it cut into the skin of black women, too.

Black men pulled the oxen, chopped the cotton, planted the sugar cane, tilled the fields; so did black women. The rope, the gun and the flame that the slave master used to break black men, was used to break black women, too.

But that was not all. Black women were also uniquely oppressed as women. They were raped, molested and abused by the slave master. Pregnancy bestowed no special privileges on them. There was no maternity leave, sick time or provisions for home care. They did the same back breaking work as men.

> I observed several women, who carried their young children in their arms to the field. These mothers laid their children at the side of the fence or under the shade of the cotton plants, whilst they were at work, and when the rest of us went to get water, they would go to give suck to their children....

American history has begun to record the struggle and sacrifice of black leaders, Frederick Douglass, Martin Delaney, Henry Highland Garnet, Samuel Ward, John Mercer Langston, Demark Vessey, Nat Turner and Gabriel Prosser in the anti-slavery fight. Yet those same history books often ignore the pantheon of black heroines: Mammy Pleasant, Harriet Tubman, Sojourner Truth, Frances Ellen Watkins, Sarah Forten, Ellen Craft, Maria W. Stewart, Amy Spain, Sarah Douglass, Susie King Taylor and thousands of other unnamed black women. These women took their rightful place beside their men (sometimes in front) and wrote their names in the proud tapestry of the American freedom movement.

The end of slavery did not mean freedom. During the half century after slavery the period historian Rayford Logan called the "nadir," black women endured the terror of lynching, political disfranchisement, peonage and rigid segregation laws.

> There are two kinds of females in this country—colored women and white ladies. Colored women are maids, cooks, taxi drivers, crossing guards, schoolteachers, welfare recipients, bar maids and the only time they become ladies is when they are cleaning ladies.

Black women were determined to fight alongside their men against racism. Together, they formed a true partnership against injustice. The stakes for black women were just as great as for their men. They pioneered and trailblazed new paths in education, labor, politics, social work and journalism. Mary McLeod Bethune, Mary Church Terrell, Nannie Burroughs, Charlotte Hawkins Brown, Septima Clark, Fannie Barrier Williams, Daisy Lee Bates, Margaret Murray Washington, Josephine St. Pierre Ruffin, Rosa Parks, Charlotta Bass, Fannie Lou Hammer, Ella Baker and hundreds more stamped their mark on America in the era from slavery to the Civil Rights Movement.

But there was one woman who especially stood

out. Not only for her courage, but also for taking up arms to defend black men. As editor of the *Memphis Free Press* in 1892, Ida B. Wells waged a relentless editorial campaign against lynching. She received numerous death threats. But Ida B. Wells would not be intimidated. She strapped a gun to her waist and dared anyone to attack her.

When she left the city on a business trip her enemies attacked. They destroyed her newspaper offices. But, that didn't stop her. She moved to Chicago, married a prominent attorney who shared her commitment to the civil rights struggle. Together, they continued to work for political and economic empowerment for African-Americans.

She is one of the best known. What about the hundreds of thousands of women who labored in America's shadows? They prepared food, washed clothes, cleaned houses, waited on tables, worked on farms and in factories, for little pay and much abuse. Life, for them, as Poet Langston Hughes said, was never a crystal stair.

As far back as anyone can remember, black women have labored hard in the home. The problem was, the home more often than not, belonged to someone else.

I see my own children only when they happen to see me on the streets when I am out with the children, or when my children come to the yard to see me, which isn't often because my white folks don't like to see their servant's children hanging around their premises....

Black women were fixtures in the kitchens and bedchambers of many white homes. They raised generations of white children into manhood and womanhood. They did it cheerfully with a smile, but underneath that smile there was always a hidden tear. They knew that while their employers demanded that they shower their children with care and affection, black women could not as often do the same for their own.

My mother was one of those women. I remember the long hours she worked cleaning, cooking and attending to her employer's babies. She would be away from the home for long hours. Occasionally, she would bring home a little bag filled with canned goods and some meat wrapped in tin foil, or some worn clothes that her employer gave her.

She was lucky. She could go home. Several of the mothers of my friends were also domestics, but they were live-ins. My friends always had to stop in the middle of the games we played to rush home to do household chores. When their fathers came home they had to be there. I understood without being told that my friends had to cook, clean and sometimes fix their own dinner. We understood that they were part of something bigger, that their fathers needed them because their mothers were working and sacrificing to provide their families with the little extras.

Our mothers who worked as domestics were proud women. They did not consider what they did as servile or demeaning. They did not think that their employers were any better than black folks because they were white, wealthy and lived in big houses. My mother often said to me, "Always look the world squarely in the eye. You're just as good as any other man."

Despite the strength of my mother and the other black women like her, many white and black men still had a confused view of black women. They called them "Sapphire," "ho," "bitch," "broad," "thing" and "stuff" for her alleged crudity, dominance and sexual looseness. At the same time, they regaled her as "Brown Sugar," "Sepia Siren," "Black Diva," "Satin Doll," and "Ebony Queen" for her elegance, style and talent.

She has battled a legion of myths. Myths such as: She is "freer" than black men. She has more "opportunities" than black men. She doesn't need the black man. She is out to "get" the black man. She holds the black man back. According to these myths, she is seen as less of a competitive threat than the black man in business and the professions. So she will get a job quicker than a black man. In the home, she is seen as not providing emotional support or recognition of her man.

In this book, *Black Fatherhood II*, black women have their opportunity to express themselves. They say those who believe these myths are either ignorant of the realities of the lives of black women or are trying deliberately to spread discord between black men and women. They say that those who depict them as the cunning, conniving, calculating foe of the black man are guilty of perpetuating the ancient myths of the "evil" black woman.

The words spoken by the women in *Black Father-hood II* about their men are sometimes tender, sometimes harsh. Their memories are sometimes gentle, sometimes bittersweet. They have experienced the depths of broken dreams and shattered illusions, but they have also experienced the high vistas of male strength and stability. They have been buffeted by the emotional storms of life. But they have never abandoned hope. They believe in their men. They speak with conviction about the problems and possibilities of African-American men.

Their words serve as both a plea for understanding and a message of hope. The black women in this book want to preserve what is best in African-American males. They pay homage to the generations of black men who have preserved the proud tradition of strength and responsibility. These are the men that they have respected. These are the men that they have loved.

In *Black Fatherhood II*, five black women talk about their men. Their names have been changed to protect their privacy. I will let them introduce themselves.

* * * * * * * * * *

My name is Andrea. I am twenty-six years old. I was born and raised in San Francisco. I work as a publicist for a book publishing company. While I have never been married, I have a five-month-old son. Also, my fiancee has two children from a previous marriage.

I didn't really know my father. He and my mother separated right after I was born. While I talk with him occasionally, I find myself straining to find things to talk about with him. I feel a deep loss for the years I did not get a chance to really know him.

* * * * * * * * * *

My name is Rosetta. I am thirty-one years old. I was born and raised in Washington, D.C. I have never been married. However, I have come close twice. I work for a private agency that provides counseling and services for single mothers. This has made me much more sensitive and aware of the problems poor black women have with public and welfare agencies.

As a child, I lived with my mother and my stepfather. Years after my stepfather died, I got a call from my real father. It was a shock to hear from him. We've talked several times, but I can't say much has come of it.

* * * * * * * * * *

My name is Carla. I am thirty-six years old. I was born in Dayton, Ohio and grew up in California. I work as a department store manager. I have been married and divorced twice and have a nine year old daughter. The last couple of years I have taken myself out of the dating game. My concerns now are the development of my daughter and improving my spiritual and intellectual well-being.

My father and my mother separated when I was eight. Mostly what I know about him is what I heard others say. He seemed to be a man that others respected. He lives on the east coast and I don't get a chance to talk with him much. But I have to admit, one of my happiest moments was when he flew to California for my first wedding.

* * * * * * * * * *

My name is Melanie. I am forty-two years old. I was born in Milwaukee and moved to Los Angeles when I was ten. I work as a social worker for Los Angeles County. I have been married for seven years and I have a son who is six years old and a daughter who's sixteen years old. I lived with her father for two years. We were never married.

Even though my father and mother were together, he was a very distant man who didn't get involved with my life. As I've grown older, we've become more comfortable with each other. I would say that we have now become good friends.

* * * * * * * * * * **

My name is Carmen. I am fifty-four years old. I was born in Chicago and lived there for thirty years until I moved to San Diego. I work as a buyer for a furniture company. I have been married twice and have two grown sons by my first marriage. I have been married to my current husband for eleven years. I only have fleeting memories of my father. He and my mother separated when I was very young. And he died when I was a teenager. He worked as a sharecropper in Alabama. Although he was dirt poor, he tried to do the best he could to provide for us.

* * * * * * * * * **

The interview with Nina Brown and Althea Brown, the mother and grandmother, respectively is the author's memory of the past.

1
THE FATHER MYSTIQUE

I can't remember my mother ever talking about her father. Of course, it probably says something about me that I never asked her about him either. It wasn't lack of interest or indifference. It just didn't occur to me until much later that my mother had a father, too. I later learned that he had left my grandmother when my mother was fairly young. So my guess is that her memory of him was fuzzy.

He might have remained a complete mystery to me. Except, one day, I was looking at an old family album and I ran across a picture of him. It must have been taken in the years just before World War I. He was tall, light-complexioned and he was dressed in the fashion of the day, a three-piece suit coat, vest and tie with a stick pin in the collar.

I doubt whether he was actually dressed for any important occasion. In those days, African-American men put on their finest every chance they got. That was especially true when they knew they would be photographed. It was as if they knew that their picture would make an indelible imprint on the pages of time. Black men had to look their best.

I stared for a long moment at this man, my mother's father. For an instant I had a strong urge to know what kind of man he was. In that moment, I regretted that I never asked my mother about him. I wondered what she would have told me.

CARMEN: *I only saw my father two or three times a year. During his visits, he would talk to me about the farm he worked on and its animals. He would encourage me to keep up my studies and to be 'a good girl.' I don't know about my mother, but I always looked forward to his visits.*

Thinking About Him

Fathers want their sons to be tough and aggressive. They want their sons to act like real men. And real men are careful never to put their emotions on display. The father-son relationship can be the perfect male training ground for learning emotional distancing.

With daughters, it's different. Daughters are their father's little princesses. Fathers adore their daughters and want to protect them. Fathers are careful about their daughters' feelings and boast that someday they will break many men's hearts.

At times, many fathers show two different personalities with their sons and daughters. They become Mr. Hyde with their daughters and Dr. Jeckyll with their sons. With daughters, fathers are not burdened by the ego wars that rage between men. Most fathers don't turn encounters with their daughters into contests for dominance or a test of wills.

Daughters are their gentle alter-egos. They are the persons with whom they can relax and even be allowed to show their warmth and affection without being thought of as "weak." What daughter couldn't love a man like this?

ROSETTA: *My stepfather was more like a mother than a father. I say that because he did a lot of things that I thought mothers did. He took me to school and picked me up from there. He attended most of the school functions. He helped me with my homework and he did a lot of the cooking and cleaning. He was gentle, soft-spoken and always a good listener.*

Writer Pauli Murray comes to mind when I think

about daughters and their fathers. In her autobiography, *Song in a Weary Throat*, she tells what happened when her mother died. Her father decided to send her and her five brothers and sisters to live with relatives. This was not uncommon among blacks. If one or both parents either couldn't or wouldn't take care of their children, relatives would step in. This was part of the extended family, and could be traced back to the old African tradition of communal caring for children.

I don't know whether Pauli Murray understood then why her father did what he did. I do know that she was not bitter toward him. She simply said: "He was too stricken to cope with our future." She didn't really know him, but he still remained a man worth emulating.

ANDREA: *Even though I really don't know my father, I always envisioned him as tall, handsome, powerful and dependable. I thought that was the way that you were supposed to see your father.*

When sociologists spoke of the vanishing black family during the first century after slavery, they really meant black men. They spent millions of government and foundation research dollars, produced reams of reports and studies, and wrote countless articles in newspapers and magazines. In recent years, some sociologists and "family experts" have even made a lucrative career for themselves trashing the black family on TV talk shows.

Sociologists told the same story. Black men didn't take care of their families. The totally absent father was the cause of all the social problems that plagued African-Americans. The absent black man/father remained one of America's most enduring myths. The myth got started during African captivity and slavery. Most assumed that slavery permanently shattered the black family. On the surface it seemed that way. Many black family members were torn from each other and sold away to other plantations. Marriage was not legally sanctioned. And the slave master certainly did not encourage sexual chastity on the plantation.

Most historians also bought this myth. It might have stayed that way, except that a few researchers began to take a second look at the black family during slavery and the immediate period that followed. They checked journals, diaries, logs, personal memoirs, county records and bills of sales. To their surprise, they found that the black family was not totally obliterated. Many fathers were there and their children remembered them.

MELANIE: *My father worked nights. So I didn't see him that much. Once, I had to do a school paper on a dancer. I mentioned it to my father because I knew that he was a big music lover. Shortly after that, it was about two or three o'clock in the morning and he came into my room and woke me up. He took my hand and led me into the living room. On*

the TV, I saw the dancer being interviewed. I was shocked.
We sat there together on the couch watching the interview.
I was surprised that he remembered. I felt so proud and so
close to him.

That was the past. Today, too many black women
tell of broken homes, broken dreams and just plain
being broke. And they're right. Fewer than half of all
black women live with their husbands. The separation
and divorce rate is higher among blacks than whites.
And the teen pregnancy rate is seven times higher for
black girls than whites.

What many don't know is that the black single
parent home is very recent. In 1970, seven out of ten
black fathers were in the home. In 1980, nearly six out
of ten black men were in the home. Now let's do
something sociologists rarely do when studying the
black family. Let's compare apples to apples. If you
take black families with income, assets and professions
that match those of white families, you will find that
the same number of black men stay in the home as
white men.

Also, many black women say that most of the black
fathers that have left the home still maintain some
contact with their children, and provide some money,
food or clothes if they can.

If they didn't, how could so many women have
such fond remembrances of their fathers? The stories
they tell couldn't entirely be spun from their dreams or

imagination.

CARLA: *The small town we lived in didn't have that many blacks. My father felt that it was important that a black man should not let color stand in the way of getting ahead. I later found out that he ran for city council several times. He always fought for promotions where he worked. Eventually, he attained one of the highest positions a black man had gotten in the company. I could tell that people looked up to him. It seemed wherever I went, they were always talking about him.*

I ALWAYS THOUGHT YOU WERE SUP-POSED TO SEE YOUR FATHER AS TALL, HANDSOME, AND DEPENDABLE.

"At this point, the present tangle of pathology is capable of perpetuating itself without assistance from the white world." More than a quarter century later those words from then sociologist Daniel Patrick Moynihan still cause much anger among African-Americans, and resentment among many white Americans. Moynihan was talking about the black family.

In his 1965 report, *The Negro Family: The Case for National Action*, he based his famous indictment of African-Americans on the dubious conclusion that one in four black men had abandoned their families.

Even if true, that still meant that three out of four black fathers were still in the home. These men, who for the most part, led quiet, perhaps even non-descript lives, were tremendously important, too. Who were they? What did they do? What kind of lives did they lead? What kind of fathers were they? Some of them must have done something right. Why didn't Moynihan talk about them? Didn't they deserve more than a passing footnote?

CARMEN: *Even though my father was a sharecropper, he always left my mother some money when he visited. The way I knew this was because after he left, we had more to eat and I always got a new dress. This meant a lot to me.*

Idols and Illusions

Many girls see their fathers as princes with grace and charm who can soothe and comfort them in times of need or pain. Other girls liken their fathers to the mythical Greek hero, Heracles (better known by the Roman name, Hercules). In the fabled story, Eurystehus, the king of Mycenae, was so jealous of Hercules that he ordered him to perform twelve impossible tasks. One of them was to clean the filth from the massive Augeias stables. The king, of course, didn't realize the superhuman powers Hercules possessed. Hercules easily performed the task in one day by diverting the waters of two rivers through the stables. It was a task beyond the capacity of a mere mortal.

Like Hercules, many girls believe their fathers have the capacity to successfully cleanse the evil from the mythical Augeias stables of America. To a large degree, men are seen this way because American society, until very recently, has assigned rigid gender roles to men and women. Men were slotted into the carefully defined role of family provider, protector and pillar of strength. Yet trying to be all these things is a terrible burden for most men to bear. Fathers are truly prisoners of the unrealistic desires that society places on men.

ANDREA: *The few times that I see my father now, I can't think of much to talk about. He may ask me about my job, or if I have enough money. But it never goes beyond just surface things. When I try to talk about something I think might interest him, I don't get any response from him.*

Black men are doubly trapped. They can't escape the demands of fatherhood, exaggerated and unrealistic though they may be. The father's role has been worked out through centuries of male privilege. This privilege was based on the greater natural strength, stamina and courage that men supposedly possessed. In times past, men were expected to hunt, trap, fight the battles, guard the cave and protect the tribe.

Several millennia later, the rules gradually changed.

Still, those who cling to the "old values" demand that men fulfill their duties as guardians of the tribe. Now instead of hunting, fishing and trapping they must have an education, profession and earn big $$$$$.

Yet while society constructs its myths about fatherhood, it also constructs its barriers. During the era of legal segregation, many colleges and universities refused to admit black students. Corporations refused to hire and promote black workers. Many labor unions refused to recruit and organize black laborers. Black mothers anxiously watched as their men took to the road in search of a better life for their families. Even today, the unemployment rate, according to official government figures, for black men chronically hovers at twice that of white men.

Maybe we shouldn't be totally surprised when some black fathers fall short of our expectations.

ROSETTA: *It's hard to admit it. But from what I could tell from listening to my mother, it seemed that my father was the type of man who avoided making decisions. He was good at making promises that he didn't keep. I don't know why he did this, but I know that it made it hard for me to know him and respect him.*

For many years, my sister and I called it "the ice cream bowl incident."

It started innocently enough. My mother asked my

father to put his ice cream bowl in the sink. A simple request that ninety-nine out of one-hundred times would not have merited any thought. This time it was different.

My father took offense. I don't know why. Maybe he was under pressure at work. Maybe they were having financial problems. Maybe he just felt as though there were too many "maybes" in his life. What happened next couldn't have had anything to do with a bowl of ice cream.

My sister and I stood and watched as they began shouting at each other. This quickly escalated into pushing and shoving. I don't believe my father intended to physically harm my mother. The only things injured were their feelings.

But their fight had an effect on my sister. She was crying and pulling at my father imploring him to stop. That happened nearly forty years ago, but to this day, I still see the fear and hurt on my sister's face. In that moment when his powder keg of anger inside him exploded in the face of his daughter, what did she think? Did he lose some or all of the esteem in which she held him?

MELANIE: *My father was always busy with his work and never had enough time for me. I would listen to my friends talk about their fathers and the things that they did with them and I would feel jealous and sad. I would hope even harder that my father would take the same interest in me as my friend's fathers did with them.*

One of the deep tragedies of American society is that circumstances such as poor education, unemployment and alcoholism, prevent many men from nurturing and caring for their children. For them, life is a desperate battle for survival. Rather than battle back, they give up, and when they do the casualties are often the ones who are closest to them and love them.

Off the Pedestal

Today, we see them everywhere. They sleep on bus stop benches, sidewalks and in parks. They push shopping carts overflowing with cans, bottles and newspapers down city streets. They accost us on street corners, in front of stores and offices begging for spare change. They offer to wipe our windows and pump our gas. They hold up signs on street corners and freeway off-ramps that read "will work for food." Many of us speak about them in embarrassed, even hushed terms.

Depending on whose figures you believe, there maybe as many as seven million of them. They are the homeless and they have become a permanent feature on America's landscape. Racism and poverty have driven many black men to the streets. And sadly, many of them are our fathers.

CARLA: *It's a strange feeling. One day your father is there and the next day he's gone. The man that I looked up to and admired for the things he did, was no longer a part of my life. No one explained anything to me. He just wasn't there anymore. I was too young to ask questions or even to know the questions to ask. But I knew that my life had changed, and I didn't know why.*

She is a very close friend. There were few things that we didn't discuss openly and honestly. Yet there was one thing with which she seemed to be obsessed: her father. Her parents had either divorced or separated when she was very young and her mother didn't say much to her about him. This is not unusual. Often, when the father leaves home, his wife will erect a wall of silence around him. It's almost as if the father is banned to a nether world never to emerge for his children to have a chance to know anything about him.

As she got older, she began to question her mother about him. The answers she got were vague and evasive. If she pressed too hard, her mother would become irritated and close the discussion with a curt word or a look of disdain. She learned that her father was a taboo subject. This only made her more curious about him.

ANDREA: *Even now, I still want him to touch me, to reach out and hug or embrace me. I want him to show warmth and affection toward me. I want to feel like I really mean something to him and that he really cares about me. So far, he hasn't done this and I haven't asked him to do it.*

Unable to break through the wall of silence about him, my friend did the next best thing. She used her imagination. She carefully constructed a imaginary fairyland in which her father became larger than life. Each day she dreamed that he would greet her with a kiss and hug as he came home from work. In the evening, she would sit next to him in a big chair by a warm fire as they read stories together. They would spend many warm summer afternoons together at the park. He would push her on the swing and she would shout with delight.

Now she was grown. She had her degrees, earned a substantial income and had a solid profession. Now she was determined to find this man that she dreamed about. When she questioned older relatives, she got only hazy answers.

Then she hired a private investigator. It didn't take him long to locate a sister of her father. After a couple of phone conversations, her aunt told her that he had died a few years earlier. How? She asked several times. There was silence. And then her aunt politely ended the conversation. My friend didn't let it go at that. She had to know so, she went to visit her aunt. After a lengthy talk, her aunt finally admitted that he had died an alcoholic. There it was. The brutal truth. But it didn't matter. She still had her dream.

ROSETTA: *My stepfather always made sure we had food and clothes and he tried to involve himself in my life. He's been dead for many years, but that memory of him still stays with me.*

Even when reality intruded on my friend's dream world, she still thought the best about her father. But other women don't. In their imaginations, the fathers that they didn't know become demons and dragons, not princes and dragon-slayers. Some black men and women say that at an early age some black girls learn to view black men negatively.

They listen to their mother's remarks, and see them make gestures or facial expressions that convey their bitterness and anger toward the fathers who abandoned the home. For some women this is an understandable reaction to the personal pain and financial hardship they may have experienced trying to be both mother and father to their children.

Still, the questions are: Do some mothers inadvertently plant the seeds of doubt about black men? Does this explain why so many black women later have problems in having a meaningful relationship with a black man? Do they see in black men an ugly reflection of their father?

CARMEN: *Children want to know both of their parents. They need to have the chance to make up their own minds about their fathers. Most children genuinely want to know who he is and what kind of man he is, especially if they haven't had much contact with him. As they get older, it's natural for them to question their mother about him. If the mother hasn't got anything positive to say about him, then children become even more curious. They become skeptical. In time, the children may come to resent both the mother and the father.*

> EVEN NOW I WANT MY FATHER TO REACH OUT AND HUG ME. I WANT TO FEEL LIKE I MEAN SOMETHING TO HIM.

The bible admonishes us to put away childish things when we become adults. Most black women have done that with their fathers. With the passage of time, many black women have managed to come to grips with reality. They have discovered that their father was neither a saint nor a sinner. Whether he succeeded or failed as the man they dreamed him to be, he still remains their father. And, for many, that is enough.

For other women, who really never knew their fathers, that isn't enough. In the quiet moments, they would still wonder what their lives might have been if their fathers had been there for them.

2
LOOKING FOR "MR. RIGHT"

Many black women think that it's easier to find the holy grail, fountain of youth or the city of gold than to find HIM. Jazz and Blues singers Bessie Smith, Billie Holiday, Big Mama Thornton, Dinah Washington, Ella Fitzgerald, Lena Horne, Nancy Wilson, Roberta Flack, Etta James, Tina Turner, Anita Baker and Whitney Houston have sung about HIM. Playwrights and novelists write about HIM. Artists draw pictures of HIM. Mothers and grandmothers tell their daughters about HIM. Their daughters tell their daughters about HIM.

Who is this man. He's Mr. Right. He's the idealized, nearly legendary figure, who many women desire. He embodies romance and perfection. He displays elegance and style. He is gentle and kind. He is successful and goal-oriented. He can slay dragons and topple giants. He's the man that every mother dreams their daughter will bring home. When they don't, many women simply say, "a good man is hard to find."

ROSETTA: *My stepfather was a very strong, self-made man. He had his own business. He provided for his family and he took an interest in his children. I want the man that I have a relationship with to have those same qualities. He shouldn't sit back and wait for something to happen. He should go out and make something happen. If he's a janitor, he should be thinking about how he can become foreman, or even start his own janitorial service.*

Princes and Cinderellas

Malcolm X knew this kind of black man was not the stuff of reality, but of a Hollywood fantasy. He wanted no part of it. In his autobiography, he tells what he and Betty Shabazz did immediately after their wedding ceremony, "I got her out of there. All of that Hollywood stuff!"

Malcolm believed that many marriages failed because of the fairy tale expectations many black women have of black men. Instead of their man taking them to dinner, dancing, kissing and hugging her every day; Malcolm noted, they got mad when their "poor, scraggly husband came home tired and sweaty from working like a dog all day, looking for some food."

Malcolm may have been a little harsh on black women. After all, many of them work hard too, and they are probably as entitled as any one else to harbor a romantic fantasy or two. But one thing is certain, like Malcolm, when American society thinks of a black man they do not think of him as Prince Charming.

CARLA: *I don't require that a man have all the answers. I think it's more important that he should set goals and try to attain them. He shouldn't back away from a challenge. He should also not be afraid to ask for help. I think a lot of men think that its a sign of weakness or failure if they ask for help. The successful man, I think, is not one who asked for help, but knows where to get the help when he needs it.*

Flowers, candy, candlelight dinners and lots of hugs and kisses may not have been on Malcolm's agenda, but such treatment is still on the agenda for many black women. When *Ebony* magazine asked dozens of single (and married) black women what they wanted in a man, they said romance.

ROSETTA: *I may be old-fashioned in saying this. But I like getting candy, flowers, or a card, and having a man compli-*

ment me on the way I look or the dress I'm wearing. I don't feel that wanting this makes me submissive or compromises my independence and assertiveness. I consider these things gestures and expressions of caring and affection. I think that women can do these things for men, too.

Some years ago, a popular magazine asked its mostly middle-class female readers if they would consider this man a suitable mate:

He's not a doctor or a lawyer: he's a bus driver.
He doesn't have a college degree.
He does not drive an expensive foreign car.
He does not like to go to restaurants or shows.
He is overweight.
He is kind, courteous, warm and attentive.
How many black women would answer "yes"?

CARMEN: *Doctors and attorneys don't impress me. Many of them can't manage their money and are in debt too. Just because a person has money doesn't mean that they are a better person. Bus drivers and garbage collectors make decent salaries, and aren't those steady jobs where a man can advance?*

I stared in disbelief at my mother, I couldn't believe what she said: "You know if anything happened to your father, I don't think I'll get married again. I'll just live with a man." Even though we had developed an easy relationship over the years, and she never hesitated to express her thoughts about the world, I was still taken back by her frank admission.

She was part of a generation where women could not even say the word "sex" out loud. In the pseudo-Victorian climate of her day, the highest aspiration that women were expected to have was to find the right man, get married, have kids and settle down to an Ozzie and Harriet life of peaceful bliss. That was the American way.

Marriage was sacred. And it was considered downright unladylike for a woman to admit that she would put romance and adventure in a relationship before home and family. Over the next few years, I often thought about her words. In time, I applauded them. Why, she was saying, should men alone define and control a relationship? Wasn't a woman entitled to have a relationship in which she made some decisions too? It was her break with the restraints and hypocrisies of the past.

ANDREA: *I want someone who is interested in my opinions and thoughts and doesn't just take me for granted.*

Jim blurted out "if she loves the car so much, then let her go make love to it." I could understand his frustration. Jim drove a late model Porsche. And during the several weeks he had dated Sharon, he thought that they had developed a good relationship. Then Jim damaged the car in an accident. For two weeks, he was stuck with a small compact. He noticed that Sharon seemed uncomfortable in the car. She became easily distant and distracted when they talked.

When Jim tried to set a time for their next date, she became evasive. Shortly afterwards, they stopped dating. He always believed that it was because of the car. He was convinced that she had really fallen in love with his car, and had only feigned interest in him. Jim may have read more into her action, and expected more out of the relationship than Sharon. It was tough to make him believe that she was not interested in him as a man as opposed to a chauffeur in a fancy car. It would have been interesting to talk to Sharon to get her side of it. Most likely she would've denied that Jim's car or money had anything to do with their break-up.

Still, I'm curious to know how many Jims and Sharons there are? Like Jim, some black men accuse black women of being "gold diggers." They say that their interest in a man goes no further than his bank account, fancy apartment, expensive Porsche, silk suits and stocks of Courvoisier. Many men tell woeful tales of women who have pretended to love them and then dumped them when they lost their jobs, or were down on their luck.

The Sharons say it is not true. Money is not their yardstick for measuring a man's value. They insist that trust, caring, warmth and responsibility are still the only treasures in men that they seek. Others are realists. They say it is hard to sustain even the most loving relationship when finances are strained. For their part, the Jims of the world hope the size of their wallet won't determine their romantic fate. Most of them will never be candidates for the lifestyles of the rich and famous.

CARMEN: *It really doesn't matter to me whether he's a professional or not as long as we both are working and striving toward the same goals. If we pool our resources together and plan our spending, not only can we pay our bills, but we can also build up our savings, acquire property, and provide the little extras for ourselves and our children. We don't always have to be scratching and clawing to stay one step ahead of the bill or tax collector or wonder where our next meal is coming from. I think this is the best way to ensure that you have a good financial footing for the future.*

> I THINK IT'S VERY IMPORTANT THAT A MAN SET GOALS AND TRIES TO ATTAIN THEM.

Crossing the Color Line

I don't remember when I first heard it, but over the years I have heard it said many times, "The two freest people in America are the black woman and the white man." As I better came to understand the plight of the black woman, I thought that if she were free it was probably news to her.

The notion that black women have somehow attained a privileged status in America probably began in slavery. Many mistook the seemingly easy sexual relationships that black women had with the slave master as a sign that he regarded her as more of a human being and less a work horse than black men.

If she were treated differently on the plantation, it was due to the slave master's greed and sexual lust. In the years that followed, if she were less likely to be beaten, lynched, jailed or unemployed than black men, it was because of the contempt that many white men held for the "weaker sex" and the fear they had of black men as social and economic competitors.

Still, old myths die hard. In *Soul on Ice*, Eldridge Cleaver could still write, "she who yearns to be rocked in the white arms of Jesus will burn for the blue eyes of and white arms of the all-American boy." Many still think that in the pursuit of her "freedom," white men in her eyes are the premium prize.

CARLA: *I have two problems with white men. One, I can't get past the looks. By that I mean most white men aren't physically appealing or attractive to me. The other problem is that I just don't think that white men can understand what black women have to go through in their lives. And, if they don't understand that, they can't give me the emotional support that I need.*

Perhaps nothing generates more emotional sparks than interracial romance. When black men fall in love with non-black women, they are sometimes called "traitors" and "sell-outs." When black women fall in love with white men, they are called "traitors," "sell-outs," AND "shameful." Shameful? Yes, because if a black woman has a relationship with a white man, many black men are ready to pin a Scarlet letter on her chest. She committed the cardinal sin of giving her body to the enemy. Many black women resent this, especially when they don't hear many of these same black men complain when black men date or marry white women.

ROSETTA: *I feel sad when I see a black man and a white woman together. It tells me that he is losing hope in himself and black women. If you question a black man about it, he turns it around and blames you. He says that black women have "bad attitudes" and "hassle you too much." He says that white women will do anything he says do. I would ask him: Do you want a woman you can control rather than a woman you can work together with to build a solid relationship?*

There may be another reason why black men complain about black women dating and marrying white men. Black men and women have frequently observed that the black women who white men marry are usually the *creme-de-la-creme* among black women. They match them in taste, sophistication, style and professional accomplishment. As one black woman put it, "she's someone who made him reach across racial lines."

Many black women say that's not always the case with black men and white women. The "forbidden fruit" syndrome still weighs heavily on too many black male-white female encounters. The income or looks of a white woman matters less to some black men than her white skin. As one black woman bitterly said, "You can stick a blond wig on a sign post and some black man will propose to it."

MELANIE: *I think black men should look a little closer at themselves and their motives when they get involved with a white woman. I wonder if they are with them because they have a real emotional feeling toward them or they see white women as status symbols?*

Or maybe a white woman is an easy way for a black man to avoid having a meaningful relationship with a black woman. If there are sincere emotional feelings, then I think that a black man and a white woman shouldn't be seen or treated any different than any other man and woman. But, if the feeling isn't there, their relationship is suspect.

The sexual war of words has taken a big toll among African-Americans. Yet emotions can't always be regulated, or turned on and off like an electric blanket. Ideally, most people fall in love with whom they want. They should be bound only by the limits of their feelings, not by a racial code. But there will always be those who will try to police the bedrooms and marriage altars of others. They do it in the name of keeping the enemy away from their women and men.

CARMEN: *I'm comfortable with a black man. I don't have to worry about what I say or do. I can just be myself and not have to feel that I have to impress somebody.*

Exactly how many black women cross the color line to date white men is uncertain. But the Census Bureau does tell us how many blacks and whites marry each year. In 1970, there were 65,000 interracial marriages. By 1990, the number had jumped to 211,000. About three out of ten of those marriages were of black women to white men.

As the numbers continue to climb, does this mean that more black women reject black men? Many men think so. Some black women candidly say that white men are more tender, sympathetic and considerate. They complain that black men are often more abusive and irresponsible. Some feel that the emotional price is too great to adhere to someone else's racial standard. If black man/white woman and black woman/white man relationships are reduced to one upmanship, we're all in trouble.

MELANIE: *Marriage is a personal choice. The black and white couples I know that have managed to stay together have been friends before they were lovers. They also worked hard to get their parents and relatives to accept them. This gave them a good start.*

There's a great scene in Spike Lee's film, *Jungle Fever* where a black executive takes his white girlfriend to a Harlem restaurant. When he tries to order, he is ignored by the black waitresses. Exasperated by the treatment, he angrily shouts to the waitress, "Why are you ignoring me?" Men want to know if there is a double standard at work. When they date a white woman, some of the hardest, most hostile stares they get are not from white men, but from black women. They try to ignore them, but, the muttered curses, complaints and snide remarks do hurt. Are white women and black men together that much of a threat to some black women?

CARLA: *It doesn't matter whether it's a man or a woman. I think interracial dating, and certainly marriage, puts too much pressure on both the man and the woman. For me, it wouldn't be worth it.*

I'm sure that the principal of the high school my mother attended thought he was doing my mother a favor when he called her into his office. He got right to the point. He suggested that she consider "passing for white." My mother was so fair complexioned that she could have easily passed. There were only a handful of black students in the school.

In those days a white skin automatically conferred special privileges on you. She wouldn't have to fear racial violence and attacks. She wouldn't have to live in an all-black neighborhood. She would not have been barred from restaurants, hotels, libraries and parks. She would have received more pay for working in a plant or factory.

There were many hard working and prosperous black men for her to marry, and successfully raise a family. But if she had married a white man with a profession or a business, she would have been assured the comforts of a good income and a stable home. She could have written her own ticket and nobody would ever have been the wiser, nobody, that is, except her.

She thanked the principal for his concern, but told him that she was "colored" and proud of it. The man she did marry—my father—was not fair-skinned, he was brown-skinned. She was especially proud of that.

ROSETTA: I *don't think it's possible for a black man or woman to be white. Or a white man or woman to be black. If they marry they are going to have to try and change their lifestyles and conform to one side or the other and they are going to have a lot of problems.*

What isn't suspect are the children of interracial marriage. They exist and their feelings have to be considered, too. The question is, "Does an interracial marriage affect the children"? Some say the children are caught in the squeeze between two hostile worlds. Yes, there will be the occasional taunts from their classmates and the thoughtless words of adults. As with most things it comes down to the two individuals. Children are a reflection of their parents. If the parents are mature, self-confident and aware, the children should develop the same maturity, self-confidence and awareness.

IF THERE AREN'T ANY SINCERE FEELINGS BETWEEN A BLACK MAN AND A WHITE WOMAN, THEIR RELATIONSHIP IS SUSPECT.

ANDREA: *I think black women and men have a responsibility to perpetuate the black race. There are a lot of talented, educated and professional black women out there. If a man tries hard enough, he can find a suitable black woman to marry and raise a family properly. A black woman can find the same kind of man. They can't just throw up their hands and say they don't exist.*

Black women may disagree over who *Mr. Right* should be or even what color he should be, but they are virtually unanimous on one thing. They want him to treat them with dignity, and, yes, respect.

Is Respect Enough

Aretha Franklin didn't want anyone to miss the point. So, in her hit recording she spelled it out "R-E-S-P-E-C-T. " She called it her "propers." That was the price this black woman demanded her man pay if he expected to win her love and allegiance. Aretha was not alone. She sang about what many black women felt. Many black men still wonder what black women mean by "their propers." It's not exactly something you can write a formula for. Nor is it as simple as specifying ingredients in a *soufflé*. What are these "propers"? Is there something that black men are missing?

MELANIE: *Many black men still don't talk to their women enough. They seem to like keeping secrets and hiding their intentions from us. This makes many black women feel that black men don't trust them enough to take them into their confidence. And women resent this.*

"Propers" to one woman may not be the same "propers" to another. Women, despite what many black men believe, do not think, feel and act as one. And even if they did the individual conditions and situations that women find themselves in with men are constantly changing. Their emotions, sentiments and needs can change, not just from day-to-day, but, from moment-to-moment.

ROSETTA: *For a while, I was seeing two different men, not because I was playing the field, but because each of these men were different types. One was soft-spoken, attentive and liked to discuss issues. The other was rugged, tough and just liked to have fun. They each fulfilled a need of mine that the other couldn't. I didn't feel I was cheating since each one knew that he wasn't the only man in my life.*

The quality of a relationship can often be gauged by something as seemly simple as the little gestures, words and even body language between two people. Take my grandmother, for instance. I don't know what kind of relationship she had with my grandfather, since I never saw them together. But, I do know how she treated my uncle. They lived together in a small house in Quincy, Illinois.

During the summers I visited them. I can remember the hot nights that they sat rocking together in the swing on the front porch. My grandmother always made sure there was a pitcher of iced tea or lemonade on a small stand by the swing. On the few occasions he would flash his temper about something that happened that day, grandmother would gently chide him and they would end up laughing together.

The bond between them was woven of love and respect. Her actions told me the meaning of respect. It was the little things captured in the small gestures, the gentle words, and their serene expressions. It was her way of telling him that he was important to her.

ANDREA: *I want the man I'm with to be as committed to our relationship as I am. I am willing to put out and do the extra things necessary to make it work. If I am willing to pick up his laundry, make a bank deposit for him, take him to work if he's having car trouble, then I want him to be willing to do the same things for me.*

Respect is a double edged sword that cuts both ways. To get it you must give it. And this is where a problem comes in. Far too many black women are willing to think the worst about their men. Even those women who should know better. When dozens of women—some married, some single—were asked if black men are irresponsible, exploitive and "act like dogs," the majority either "agreed" or "strongly agreed" with the statements. Worse, the negative things that black women believe about black men greatly out-number the negative things that black men believe about black women.

CARLA: *I think black men and women should be tired of name calling and blaming each other for the other's problems. Both sides have said and written enough to make each other feel worthless. If they spent half that time trying to figure out what each one wants and be willing to take a step toward each other, then maybe we can get somewhere.*

IF I AM WILLING TO PUT OUT AND DO THE
EXTRA THINGS FOR HIM, I WANT HIM TO
DO THE SAME FOR ME.

The Numbers Game

When a Harvard study in 1987 proclaimed that
women over age thirty had a greater chance of being
killed by a terrorist bomb than of finding a husband,
many women were furious. They said that this was yet
another example of the undeclared war on them by the
male establishment. Those who opposed women's
rights were continuing to assail and belittle them every
chance they got. The idea was to make a woman so
desperate for a man that she would rush to trade her
attaché case and business cards in for an apron and
dust mop.

Many refused to admit that they were at a disad-
vantage when it came to finding men. They said they
did not have to pound the streets or haunt the bars to
find a man. Nor, did they have to lower their standards, or compromise their principles, to keep a man.

Many black women were not amused by the debate. For them, the issue of the "male shortage" was
more than just a polite parlor debate. It was a bitter
reality.

ANDREA: *There's nothing wrong with black women going out with a man who may have been in jail, or may have a problem with drugs or alcohol. If he's a man that's really trying to get his life together, then they shouldn't be afraid to try and have a relationship with him.*

The figures tell the tale. For every ten unmarried black women past age thirty, there are seven black men. By age forty the number falls even faster. Why? Because one out of four black men are in prison, on parole or on probation. One in twenty-five black men are homicide victims. Black men suffer higher rates of cancer, heart attack, hypertension and strokes than white men. Black men have been called an "endangered species." And many black women are worried that their relationships could also be called endangered.

ROSETTA: *I think most black women are willing to give black men the benefit of the doubt. If he makes a mistake, or even if he royally screws up, they will likely forgive him. Many black women aren't dumb and they know that even though they have as many problems and needs as a man, they still will love him if he will give them a chance.*

I was part of a group of twenty or so persons that sat in the small room. We chattered loudly as we waited for the weekly meeting of the singles group to which I belonged to begin. The group was a good mix of professionals, businesspersons and blue collar workers. Two or three of them were aspiring actors and entertainers.

The sessions were divided into two parts. The first was a roundtable type discussion on some political or social topic of interest. The discussions were generally lively. Often there were sharp exchanges within the group. In the second session, a man and a woman would engage in role playing on some spicy issue. But this was only window dressing. We weren't there to spout our opinions, but, to find a man or a woman.

There were two problems. The first was that many of the men and women had recently separated or divorced and they were carrying a lot of heavy baggage from prior relationships that had gone sour. It would take time, lots of it, before many of them could face the painful truths about their lives and get on with the business of building a healthy relationship with another man or woman.

The second problem was tougher. There were never enough men. Out of the twenty or so members of the group, fifteen were women. And the ratio never changed.

CARMEN: *If a woman doesn't have a man, there's nothing wrong with being alone. She can pursue her own interests and priorities. She can join clubs, church activities, take classes, read, socialize with friends, find a lot of ways to amuse herself and be a productive person.*

No one can be sure when the practice started. Through centuries of custom and tradition, polygamy became the core of social relations within West African society. An Ashanti, Ibo, Dahomey, Yoruba or Yako man had the right to take as many brides as he could care for. In modern times, Europeans and North Americans attacked it as a vestige of male domination and female subservience.

Critics in the Western society did not go deep enough and attempt to understand the complexity of the African societies that practiced it. Polygamy was not solely conceived as a system to perpetuate male dominance and gratification. It evolved principally because of the female surplus and economic necessity.

Men were killed in wars, accidents or while hunting. In a communal society where everything was shared, the women had to be sheltered and cared for. It was mandatory that the bridegroom pay a "bride price." He could pay the parents or relatives with food, beverage, livestock or firewood. Or he could help the family plant or harvest in their fields. The household was organized to facilitate shared responsibilities for food production, trade and goods management, and most importantly, child care.

Why am I discussing polygamy? Because many African-American women have seriously discussed the issue. The "male shortage" has revived their interest in the ancient practice. In some books and magazines, the pros and cons of "shared relationships" have even become legitimate items of debate. Some women openly say that it's better to have someone in your arms part-time than to be alone all the time.

CARLA: *There was a time in my life when I would lick the carpet he walked on to please him. But I found that I was always giving, giving, giving. And he was taking, taking, taking. If I had received something back for my efforts, I probably wouldn't have minded. But since I didn't, it made me feel like I was less of a person. Now I can't do that. I will still give, but I have to get something back.*

> I THINK MOST BLACK WOMEN ARE WILL-ING TO GIVE BLACK MEN THE BENEFIT OF THE DOUBT WHEN THEY MESS UP.

For many black women, the search for *Mr. Right* has been a journey of discovery. Along the way, they have explored relationships with white men, sometimes in the hope that they will succeed where others have failed. But they have discovered no matter whether the man they choose is black or white, if he's *Mr. Right* one day, he can be *Mr. Wrong* the next.

There's another reality. They are painfully aware that the gauntlet of American problems has thinned the ranks of black men. And, since most black women will not opt to marry white men, added strains are put on black male/female relationships. Many have been forced to shed their starry-eyed vision of who or what *Mr. Wonderful* should be. They have had to lower their sights and make the necessary adjustments.

In doing so, many women have found that many men do have the strength and the capacity to care, nurture and share their lives with them. This is one reward that they have reaped during their journey.

3
BEHIND, BESIDE, IN FRONT OF HIM?

It was a raucous scene in the college auditorium. A young woman rose and asked then Black Panther Party leader, Eldridge Cleaver, what the role of women should be in the Black Power movement. Cleaver did not miss a beat, he answered "prone." He was met with a torrent of hisses and shouts from the women in the audience. Others promptly headed for the exits.

Whether Cleaver expressed his own personal view or was speaking for his Party, was not clear. He did, however, reflect the thinking of many black men during the 1960s. That was a time when men routinely believed that the place of the woman was always "two steps behind her man."

When black women protested and accused men of being male chauvinist or sexist, some men retorted that it's part of "African history and tradition." The way these men read that history, men made all the decisions in society and women served dutifully.

In black organizations, men commonly would argue philosophy, set policy and plan strategy. Women would take notes, file papers and answer the telephones. The message was clear. Black women not only were second class citizens in America, they were second class citizens in the movement, too.

ROSETTA: *The man should be king of his castle. When a major decision has to be made, I would want him to discuss it with me, but if his beliefs are stronger than mine, I would defer to him.*

Behind Him?

During the 1960s, many women weren't buying that history. They knew that even in those patrilineal African societies, women held an honored place. Taking care of the children, food production and household management required great skill and organization. It was not considered by men as incidental or frivolous. Women were central to the maintenance of a smooth and orderly society.

Moreover, women understood American history. They knew that society had used every device to deny black men their manhood. Now times had changed. Black men saw opportunities to be their own men, to make their own decisions, and stamp their seal on history. Many black women were sympathetic and believed that black men should have their opportunity to lead. All they wanted was some assurance that it wouldn't come at their expense. Black men should be leaders but they must understand that black women were not the enemy. It was a tenuous balance that many women tried to walk.

CARLA: *I let my first husband make all the major decisions. He chose the school our daughter went to, how much rent we paid, how much money we spent, the kind of car we bought and even the kind of clothes that he wanted me to wear. I didn't object to it then. I trusted his judgment and was confident that he would make the right choices.*

There is a scene in Lorraine Hansberry's powerful play, *Raisin In The Sun*, about a working class black family's struggle for survival that sticks in my mind. Walter, who drives a cab for a living, and his wife Ruth are sitting at the breakfast table. Walter tries to convince his wife that his scheme to buy a liquor store with the insurance money his mother was due to receive will make them all rich.

When Ruth interrupts him in mid-sentence and tells him to eat his eggs, Walter explodes. He shouts at her that that's what's wrong with black women, they don't ever do anything to "build up their men." Ruth fires back that black women do support their men when they accomplish things. Walter, out of frustration, mumbles loudly that black men are "tied to a race of women with small minds."

Maybe that's one of the problems. Many black women question whether their Walters are truly achieving to their abilities. While many black men question whether their Ruths will support them when they try or do achieve.

ANDREA: *I try to support my man by being involved with his activities. He belongs to a club and I go to most of the events it has. Sometimes I would rather stay home or do something else, but I know it's important to him that I be with him. If that's what he needs to make him a more complete person, I'm for it.*

Sid was a good candidate for the "headstrong" award of the year. He prided himself on being able to make firm and decisive decisions. At the office, his co-workers admired him for his leadership qualities. When disputes arose, Sid stepped in immediately and settled matters quickly and resolutely. When he made a decision, rarely was it questioned or challenged. Sid always had the final word.

Sid's wife was just the opposite. She was soft-spoken and always listened carefully to what others had to say about their problems. She always approached things with diplomacy and tact. She was a good complement to Sid. She understood his personality. She knew that he had a need to be firmly in control. But she also knew that Sid always had their best interests in mind. So when there was a problem or dispute, and she felt strongly that she was right, she was at her best.

She knew exactly how to handle the situation and him. She let him do most of the talking as she knew he would. She was careful not to interrupt or challenge him. This would only result in an argument. When he finished, she quietly stated her points. Usually, they were on the mark and Sid knew it. She knew that he might protest or stomp around a little, but she was prepared to wait him out. She knew that he would see the logic in her argument. When Sid "made" the final decision, it was surprisingly close to what she wanted or had suggested they do.

CARLA: *There are ways to make a man feel like he's "a real man" and still get your way. My daughter was an example. When it came to discipline, my husband was more of a hands on person than me. I thought he was a little too aggressive. Rather than confront him directly and end up in an argument, I would leave little clippings from newspapers and magazines on child discipline around the house that agreed with my views.*

I would talk to mutual friends who agreed with me and when they came over, I would maneuver the discussion around to the subject, so that they could have their say when he was in the room. I never said a word. After a while I noticed that he was talking more to our daughter rather than punishing her every time she misbehaved.

Most black women agree that black men have had a terrible way to go. Millions were lost during African captivity and the passage to America. On the plantation, the slave master's word was the law not only in the field, but also in the family. He put the food and clothes on the table for black women and children, not the black man. He said when the black woman could rest, sing, and dance, not the black man. He said when the black woman could marry, not the black man. He said when the black woman could rest or pray, not the black man.

He could sell, beat and even kill the black woman, while the black man was helpless to act. He had to watch while the slave master stole into his cabin or took his woman up to the big house and raped or physically assaulted her.

The black man had to be taught obedience or broken into submission. The master had to break not only his spirit, but also his manhood. There was never room on the plantation for two masters.

ROSETTA: *If I had my wish, I would love to stay home and*

take care of the house and kids. I don't need to be a modern woman. If he's watching the game, I won't bother him. Even though I used to hate cooking and dishwashing because of the stigma of women in the kitchen, if that's what he wants, I'll do it.

The list of those black men who did rebel and refused to submit would fill many pages. Black abolitionist leader, Frederick Douglass tells of his day-long epic personal struggle with Covey, "the Negro breaker." The custom was when a black man was especially stubborn or rebellious, a master would send him out to a slave breaker to be "broken." Douglass was sent to Covey. After a series of beatings, Douglass challenged Covey. They fought for several hours. It was a battle of wills and the prize was Douglass' manhood, "I was a changed being after that fight. I was nothing before— I was a man now."

ROSETTA: *If I have a good relationship with a man, I don't regard doing things to please him as "selling-out" or being dominated by him. I made the decision to devote myself to the house, kids and him because I want to do it, not because I feel I have to do it.*

MANY WOMEN ARE GOOD AT FINDING WAYS TO MAKE A MAN FEEL LIKE A MAN WHILE STILL GETTING THEIR WAY.

Beside Him?

Some feminists are puzzled as to why there aren't more black women in feminist organizations? If anything, black women have suffered the most from gender discrimination. They receive less pay and fewer benefits. They have less access to health and social services. Poor black women suffer the most when state and federal governments restrict funds to public hospitals and clinics. Black women are also subjected to sexual assaults and violence. So, again, why aren't they in the front ranks of feminist organizations?

It's a good question. Black women do have much to gain from the fight for women's rights. But many are hesitant to join feminist organizations. They feel their main battle is against racism, not sexism. In this battle, their best ally is still the black man.

CARMEN: *I strongly believe that a couple should make decisions jointly. Two people should be able to sit down and talk about their needs and then come to an agreement. If one person is always making decisions for the other there's bound to be resentment and hostility. This will often come out in ways that the other doesn't see or understand.*

It was a sad spectacle for most African-Americans to watch. A black man and a black woman on national TV, swapping accusations of sexual misconduct. For days, the nation was tantalized by the charges of sexual harassment made by Anita Hill against U.S. Supreme Court Justice nominee, Clarence Thomas.

The issue was not whether Anita Hill was telling the truth. The issue was that a black woman and a black man were at odds. Many black women regard sexual harassment as a serious matter and they support penalties against it. They believe that racism and sexism (even among African-American men) are twin evils, and that both must be fought with equal vigor. But they also looked beyond Hill and Thomas at America.

African-Americans were reeling from a decade of Reagan-Bush administration assaults on civil rights, social services, education and job programs. On top of this, the problems of crime, drugs, gangs and violence were piling higher on the doorsteps of African-Americans. That's why many blacks were alarmed. They thought that the Hill-Thomas fight being played out before the eyes of racially unsympathetic whites could be used by them to further degrade blacks. Many said that this was the time for African-American men and women to unite and not fight each other.

CARLA: *I try to find out what he wants, what will satisfy him. I try to do it without nagging or making him feel like he's on the spot. I don't do this to keep the peace. I do it because I want to make myself happy. If he's not happy, there's no way that I can be happy.*

Still others wondered. If blacks continue to engage

in their bruising battle of the sexes, won't this deepen the suspicions of much of white America that there is something "pathologically" wrong with black men AND women? Bigots could then easily ask, If black men and women can't get along with each other, then why should we?

MELANIE: *I think many black men are still caught up in the need to control their women. If a woman voices opinions that may differ from his, he feels threatened, or takes it as a sign that she doesn't love or respect him. Men should stop for a moment and think how they deal with their male friends they disagree with. Do they stop being friends with them? Do they take it as a personal challenge or insult? No, they might end up going for a drink and laughing about it. They can do the same with a woman.*

Malcolm X liked to tell audiences that black people don't catch hell because they are Methodist, Baptist, Catholic or Muslim. They catch hell because they are black. His point: blackness is the great leveler in America. It cuts across all class and religious lines. No matter whether an African-American is a millionaire or a pauper, a supreme court justice or a prison inmate, a surgeon or an indigent patient, a university president or a high school drop-out. If you're black you can still be refused a loan, denied a job or promotion or be harassed by the police. Gender? It makes little difference whether it's an African-American male or female.

ANDREA: *My fiancee and I have been stopped a couple of times by the police. Both times they made us get out of the car. They asked us a lot of questions and ran checks on both of us. It didn't seem to matter to them that our children were in the car. They had these two blacks and they were going to make sure both of us were clean before they let us go.*

She's a highly paid reporter who travels frequently on assignments. On several occasions, this black woman has been frisked and questioned. She's had her purse and luggage searched and her passport inspected. She does not look like a drug dealer or a smuggler. Being a successful career woman means little. Being black means everything.

MELANIE: *In my position as a social worker, I notice that when it comes to single black mothers, case workers will, at the slightest suspicion that a mother is neglecting or abusing her children, recommend that they be placed under protective care. They hardly ever do this with white children.*

I have seen the photo many times. And I am always struck by the determined looks on the faces of Dr. Martin Luther King and his wife Coretta as they marched down the highway locked arm-in-arm. The photo was taken during the famed March from Selma to Montgomery, Alabama in 1965. Nearly twenty-five thousand people marched together that day for political justice and economic rights in America. They were the conscience and soul of America.

On that eventful day, there were many other black couples among the marchers. They had their eyes fixed firmly on history. They had their eyes firmly fixed on each other.

CARMEN: *A husband and a wife have to work at compatibility. Even then it can take many years before a couple learns each others needs, and desires. And it may take even more years before they recognize the ways that a person expresses them. One person doesn't always have to tell the other person, for example, that they want to be held, or comforted, or that they want to be left alone. They can communicate that by a look, a gesture, a smile, a frown, or even silence. When I hear that a couple is getting a separation or divorce, after say 20, 25, or 30 years of marriage, I'm convinced that many of them, despite all those years together, are in some ways probably still strangers to each other.*

I knew instantly that something was wrong. My mother sat immobile in her chair. She stared at the TV. Her eyes were ringed with deep, red circles. She had been crying. She did not look at me as I sat down. It seemed as if she was frozen in time. On the screen was a group of black men, they were hovering over the body of a prostrate man on the balcony of the Lorraine Motel.

The date was April 4, 1968. Dr. King had just been

cut down by an assassin's bullet in Memphis, Tennessee. As I watched her staring intently at the TV screen, I thought of the scene following Indian leader Mohandas Gandhi's assassination. At his funeral, distraught women tried to throw themselves on his burning funeral pyre. They had been very much a part of his life and struggle for freedom. And they wanted to be a part of him, even in death.

As King lay prostrate on the balcony with the life ebbing from him, I knew that my mother and millions of other black women were dying inside too. They deeply loved, revered and respected the man. To them, he was more than just a leader, he was a loving black man. He exemplified strength, dedication and purpose.

He was the kind of man that my mother respected and admired. He was the kind of man with whom she would be proud to stand side-by-side. Even though there would be no funeral pyre for King, the embers of the deep respect she had for him as a leader and a man would always burn in her heart.

ROSETTA: *Maybe I'm a little naive. But I want a man that I can give all my trust to. If I'm with someone and he's not worthy of my trust then I know that I won't be with him very long. And I'm pretty sure that he also wants me to be the kind of woman that he can trust too.*

Ana and Frederick Douglass, W.E. B. and Shirley

Graham DuBois, Margaret and Booker T. Washington, Marcus and Amy Jacques Garvey, Eslanda and Paul Robeson, Richard and Julia Wright, Ida B. Wells and Ferdinand Lee Barnett, and Malcolm X and Betty Shabazz. Can anyone think of better teams?

CARLA: *I couldn't stay with a man very long that I didn't respect. I want to feel that a man believes in something rather than just talking to hear himself talk.*

> I THINK MANY BLACK MEN STILL THINK THEY MUST CONTROL THEIR WOMEN. IF A WOMAN VOICES OPINIONS THAT DIFFER FROM HIS, HE FEELS THREATENED.

History provides no examples of generals winning major battles by leaving half of their army in the rear. The struggle against racism and exploitation are monumental battles. It has consumed the energies of black men and women for four centuries in America.

It is a battle that has been marked by advances and retreats, forward thrusts, and backward marches. At each step, black women nursed their men in battle, offered them their shoulders to cry on in tragedy and crisis, and extended to them their hands to lift them up when they fell. They bolstered their resolve and confidence to continue the struggle.

CARMEN: *Men try to cover up their feelings and not let you know when they hurt, because that's what the world expects them to do. But when a man gets behind the doors of his home, he will show his true feelings. If he's hurting it will come out and his woman will pick up the vibes from him that tell her he needs and wants a pat or a stroke to pick him up.*

Many black fathers understand that manhood is not adulthood. Manhood requires that a male attain responsibility, commitment and wisdom. Adulthood requires only that a male attain legal age. Manhood does not come by luck or chance. It requires patience, hard work and understanding. Many men are prepared to take their sons through the ancient African tradition called the "rites of passage" to reach manhood.

What about their daughters? Should they be left out of the process of self-actualization too? The Sojourner Truth Adolescent Rites Society believes that the same passage is necessary for girls to become women. In their rites of passage they teach:

Family History
Sex Education
History of Our People
Spirituality/Community Spirit
Taking Care of Self
Housekeeping/Finances
Assertiveness/Leadership

Values Clarification/Future Planning
Time Management/Organizational Skills
Art and Dance

First, they want to make girls conscious of their dignity and worth as women. And second, they want to make them aware of their duties and responsibilities to their communities and to their families.

MELANIE: *There's been so much emphasis on the problems of black men, that black women have gotten lost in the shuffle. That's not to say that black men don't have some serious problems, like health, prison and unemployment. But, with black women, the pressures are just as great, maybe even greater, because we're women, too.*

In Front of Him?

"Move or Die!" The tone in her voice and the cold steel of the revolver pressed to the frightened slave's head told him that Harriet Tubman meant business. Twenty-five times the frail but iron-willed woman went South. She defied dogs, night riders, slave patrols and posses. She braved the dangers of the swamps, forests and rushing rivers to deliver slaves from captivity. She prided herself on never losing a single passenger. They did not call her Moses for nothing.

When a slave signed on with her, there was no turning back.

CARLA: *I can't blindly follow anyone. I know what I want and I am just as capable as anyone of making my own decisions.*

When our daughters are children, we want them to wear pretty little dresses. We want them to help their mothers in the kitchen and around the house. We want them to come home promptly every day from school.

When they are teens, we want to know who their friends are. We want to know what they do every moment they are away from home. We want them to always act in a demure and ladylike manner. We want them to be escorted everywhere they go.

When they are adults we want them to choose the right career. We want them to pick the right husband. We want to protect our daughters from the pitfalls of the male, dominated world.

But one day our daughters will be women. They will make their own decisions and lead their own lives. On that day, the things we want may not be the things they want.

CARMEN: *As girls, many women learned how to plan, manage and organize time, money and work. It's a talent they use everyday with their families, children, relationships and on their jobs, oftentimes without knowing it.*

That day came with my daughter. I wanted her to pursue her graduate studies at a college close to home. It had a good curriculum and she would have access to a car. It made perfectly good sense to me, but, not to her.

The school she wanted to go to was on the east coast. There, she would not have a car. The courses she wanted to take were chancy, career wise, and she would have to adjust to life in a new city. She wasn't deterred. She visited the campus and liked it and then applied. She even received an academic scholarship.

My daughter loves me and she respects me. She talked to me and she listened to me, but in the end, she followed her heart and her head, made her own decision. She was a winner and so was I.

ANDREA: *A lot of men hate to ask a woman's opinion about something, until a problem or a crisis comes up. Then, they'll ask.*

If there is one word that can sum up the lives of many black women it is RESPONSIBILITY. When they were young girls, they had to follow strict rules and perform duties, often very strict. They had to help their mothers cook, clean, wash and iron. When they were teenagers, they cooked, cleaned, washed and ironed AND worked at jobs outside the home. As adults, they cooked, cleaned, washed and ironed, worked outside the home AND took care of their children and their husbands.

Nearly every moment of their lives, black women have had to make decisions. More often than not, the only ones with whom they had to keep counsel were themselves. This was not by choice. Poverty or broken homes had often forced them to be both mother and breadwinner. Many saw the role as a challenge. It was almost as if the fate of their people rested on their sometimes broad, sometimes narrow, but always weary, shoulders.

MELANIE: *A woman made decisions about her life long before she met her husband or boyfriend.*

The eight black women profiled in a popular black magazine possessed poise, confidence, talent and plenty of savvy. They were successful as corporate chief executives, public officials, business owners, attorneys and doctors.

I noted one other thing, only two of them were married. The other six were single either by choice or because of failed marriages. Why? Each of the six women clearly stated what they wanted in a mate. I couldn't help but wonder whether the very success they created for themselves made many men wary of them?

ROSETTA: *I think some women do things to push men*

away without realizing it. It may be their attitude or the way they act. That's why I think it's good to have a close friend who can act as a sounding board. They may be able to point out faults or problems that you may not see.

"She slapped me" and then she asked me, "How come yuh didn't hide." How come yuh always fightin?" For novelist Richard Wright, the memory of his mother rebuking him for daring to throw rocks at the white boys who had attacked him was painful. In the "Ethics of Jim Crow," Wright pointed to a dilemma that many black mothers and their sons have faced.

They understand that much of American society is hostile to black men. They know that too many black men have been jailed, beaten or killed for fighting back against injustice and racism.

In their tales of growing up, many black men, especially in the South, tell how their mothers scolded or punished them for talking back to whites. Some mothers probably just wanted their sons to show good manners and respect to adults. Others, like Wright's mother, may have been trying to shield them from the danger that could come to a black man who challenges white authority.

But in harnessing their son's aggression and energy, do some women in effect emasculate them? Do they prevent them from becoming the protectors and defenders of their families and communities? Do they pass the mantle of leadership to black women by default?

ANDREA: *I don't know why some men feel challenged when women make decisions. I would think that a man should be glad if a woman for a change plans a trip or activity that he would enjoy. Just like men want women to go with the flow, they should do the same. Who knows, they might like it.*

They go by various names: male bonding, men's consciousness, male self-awareness and so on. Black men form these groups to show their women that men want to be sensitive, caring and nurturing. Many are sincere about wanting to get in touch with the real essence of their manhood. They believe that women have much to show them about these qualities.

That men feel the need to join these groups is a stark admission that male domination and sexism exacts a terrible price on men just as racism does on whites. The emotional stunting from male sexual privilege prevents them from enjoying a productive and meaningful relationship with women as equal persons and equal partners. For many black women this is a welcome turn and may lead to stronger more productive relationships with men.

A WOMAN MADE DECISIONS ABOUT HER LIFE LONG BEFORE SHE MET HER HUSBAND OR BOYFRIEND.

CARLA: *I feel that most men are afraid to let themselves go. I have told men friends of mine several times, "Why don't you try hugging." It's OK to touch someone if you feel like it. Nobody will laugh at you or think you're silly.*

Is it enough for men to talk to other men? Is there a danger that men left alone to their own devices may simply reinforce their own biases and stroke their egos? If that happens, they may never discover that it's OK to: hail their woman's successes and triumphs and not feel threatened by them; make decisions with a woman and not for her; cry when they feel joy or sadness, and not suppress their feelings; replace the tattered mantle of aloofness, with the cloak of personal warmth; understand that men can be tender, gentle, compassionate and reflective and still be decisive, tough, tenacious and aggressive. They can discover what women have always known, that strength comes in many forms.

ANDREA: *When I am angry or even happy, I want him to acknowledge my feelings. Look at my facial expressions, listen to my voice, see it, recognize it and react to it. I don't want him to pretend or try to ignore that I don't have feelings too,*

Should black women stand behind, beside or in front of their men? There is no one answer. There are times when black women have chosen to do one or the other. There are times when she has chosen to do all three. It does not mean that black women are in competition with black men. Most black women prefer to think of themselves as in partnership with their men. They want their relations with them to be based on mutual respect and sharing.

Many women are still willing to put aside their momentary and emotional needs, to give their man the little extra stroke or pat on the back he needs. They know that black men assaulted for decades by American society are still in the frantic search to discover themselves and their "maleness."

They also don't want men to forget that women have their own physical and emotional needs and personal ambitions, too. Women remind men that the same pat or stroke they are willing to give them, they also need. Women want a level playing field in the relationship game.

4
I Work Hard, Too!

Mary Frances Webb's grandmother told her that she "sawed and cut cord wood just like a man." She said that it didn't hurt because she was as strong as an ox. When she finished those labors, she also "helped make all the cloth for their children and weaved hats for the men."

Fannie Moore's mother told her that after she worked all day in the fields, she would "piece and quilt all night." For these two slave women, there was no rest. By day, they worked beside their men. At night, they cooked, cleaned, sewed and did many other extra jobs. It didn't matter whether their bones ached with fatigue or they were too tired to eat. While their men rested, they still had to work at what they called their "second set of tasks."

ANDREA: *I think work should be a trade-off. If a woman can do the job, so can a man.*

Each time I watch the old news clips of life in America during World War II, I see women working as welders, assemblers and mechanics at defense plants and in shipyards. It did not mean that America had changed its opinion of women. It just meant that there were not enough men to fill the vital jobs at war plants. So, women were used. For the first time, many of them were black.

Aided by the male shortage and an executive order from President Franklin Delano Roosevelt banning racial discrimination in the defense industry, black women were able to land jobs in assembly plants at less pay. But as women, their lot pretty much remained the same. They still came home to tend to their children, prepare the meals and wash the dirty dishes.

For most black women, this was nothing new. They always had to work inside and outside the home.

CARLA: *Just because I'm a woman and you're a man doesn't mean that we have to stick to certain roles. If he's a better cook than I am, or irons better than I do, and he enjoys doing it, more than I do, that's what he should do. If I'm better at shampooing the carpets or painting, that's what I should do.*

Sharing the Burden

Each day my mother busily went about the business of doing her household chores. This was the 1950s. The men had come home from the battlefields of Europe and the Pacific. The Cold War between the United States and the Soviet Union was in full swing. Touted as an era of unlimited prosperity, the American Century had begun.

The women turned in their welder's masks and assembler's gloves and picked up their dust mops and kitchen scrub brushes again. While America nestled comfortably into its decade of political slumber, somebody had to take care of those millions of new babies that in time would come to be called "baby boomers."

I was one of those babies. Before she found a job as a domestic, my mother was one of the millions of women who stayed home to take care of their babies. People might have considered her fortunate. My father had a good job at the Post Office. In those days, for a black man, working at the Post Office was like working for a *Fortune 500* corporation. A black man holding that job was considered important and well-to-do.

On the surface, my mother had a comfortable,

contented life. But this was deceptive. As time passed and I grew older, I could tell from her complaints that she was plainly bored with the mundane routine of cooking, cleaning and household chores. She wanted to do more with her life. So she became an avid reader. She read newspapers, magazines and lots of books. She wrote letters and took correspondence courses.

She wanted to tap the well-spring of creativity hidden inside herself. From the remarks I heard my father make about women, I knew that he watched this with both curiosity and dread. He believed that women should stay home and take care of the house and children. He knew that the world was changing and that she was changing with it.

ROSETTA: *If I have to put in eight hours a day on the job, I don't think there should be any limitations on the type of work that he should or shouldn't do. If he gets home before me and the clothes need to be washed, wash them. If the rug needs to be vacuumed, don't wait for me to get home to do it. Go ahead and vacuum it.*

Have black women replaced men as the "breadwinners" in the black family? The issue has caused much debate and soul searching among many African-Americans. Many black men believe that black women are their economic competitors. They say that whites will hire black women for positions instead of black men, because they are less threatening. Black women counter that if they get hired it's because they are qualified, not because of any imagined gender one-upmanship.

Certainly black women have attained heights that would have been undreamed of by their grandmothers. During the past two decades, black women have broken down barriers in business and professions. They are entrepreneurs, tradespeople, engineers, accountants, architects, doctors, lawyers, business owners, and executives. They outnumber black males at colleges and universities. One in nine black women earn more than $25,000 annually.

But black professional women get married, too. When they come home, they take off their suits and put down their attaché cases. They have houses to clean, meals to fix and children to take care of. At that moment, their grandmothers would recognize them as women doing the same things that they did.

CARLA: *I don't think you have to draw up a schedule and say that I'll do this half and you do that half of the work. I think there are certain things that men expect women to do, like cooking and cleaning. I think most women expect they will have to do those things.*

While men are getting better at doing housework and helping in the home, the gap is still as wide as the Grand Canyon. In 1965, married women each week put in 31.6 hours of housework, men put in 4.7 hours.

In 1985, women put in 22.4 hours, men 11.1 hours. Many black women ask, "Don't I have to get up early each day, get dressed, fight traffic, put in eight long hours, too"? "Don't I bring home a paycheck, too"? "Aren't I tired and stressed out when I come home, too"? "What would happen if I played like Houdini the magician and disappeared when it came time to doing the housework"?

> JUST BECAUSE I'M A WOMAN AND YOU'RE A MAN DOESN'T MEAN WE HAVE TO STICK TO CERTAIN ROLES.

ROSETTA: *I was involved with one man who was pretty traditional. I do the housework, but he wouldn't do it. I would cook, clean and do most of the housework, but he couldn't be bothered. When I suggested that once in a while he could help me do these things, he shrugged it off. His actions told me that he regarded these things as "my job." It became too much, working and trying to cater to him too.*

It got so bad a few years ago that many women began demanding that they be paid for their housework. They calculated that since many men did not want to do their fair share at home, then why not just pay women for the work they do? After all, they said, a domestic worker gets paid for her work and a maid charges for her work. A laundress charges for her work and so does a dishwasher for her work. A baby sitter gets paid for her work. Since many women say that they do all of these things, if their husbands paid for their services, they would still be getting a bargain. It would be a package rate deal.

CARLA: *When my husband washed the dishes or did the laundry, I made it a point to tell him what a great job he had done. I would even brag about it to a relative or a friend. He would stick his chest out and beam. I thought that this would encourage him to do it more often.*

For Men Only

No person in the United States shall, on the basis of sex, be excluded from participation in, be denied the benefits of, or be subjected to discrimination under any education program....

Two decades ago, Title IX of the education amendments to the U.S. Code became law. It was supposed to guarantee the end of sexual discrimination in funding for sports and other school activities. Whatever opportunities the boys received, girls also must receive. Whatever money was spent on programs for boys, girls must also receive the same amount.

Title IX was designed to put society out of the business of gender discrimination. Optimists hoped that this regulation would have a more far-reaching social impact and encourage boys to regard girls, and ultimately, men to regard women as equals in society. At least that was the hope.

ANDREA: *It's important to me that a man offer to help me with the day-to-day things we need to do both in and outside the home. It shows that he understands and appreciates my efforts to bring in income and try to keep up the house and the children.*

The next time you pass an elementary or junior high school at the close of the school day, pause for a moment. If you look closely at the students playing in the school yard, you'll notice that most of them are boys. They are shooting baskets, tossing a football, kicking a soccer ball or just goofing off.

Many girls aren't allowed that luxury. They may live in a single parent household, usually with their mother, who must work. They may have to hurry home immediately after their final class to take care of younger brothers and sisters, clean house, wash and iron and prepare dinners. Why don't the boys rush home to do the same?

CARLA: *I knew what my duties were at home. My mother made sure of it. When she cooked, I would have to wash the dishes. When she vacuumed, I dusted. When she washed, I*

*ironed. She never had to tell me to do these things. It became
part of the routine.*

My friend Cynthia was furious. She couldn't stop
talking about it. It was her second or third date with
Warren. They had gone to a party. Things had gone
pretty smoothly. People were enjoying themselves
and Cynthia was having a good time. Until....

She and Warren were talking with two other
couples. Suddenly, Warren turned to her and asked
her to get him a drink. She felt as if she had been
slapped with a cold towel. It wasn't so much the
request. She liked him and probably would have been
happy to get him a drink. It was the way he asked that
rankled her. It sounded less like a request then a
command. She didn't think that she was being overly
sensitive either, because in the same instant he asked,
she noticed that one of the other women dropped her
eyes as if she was embarrassed for her.

Being a witty person, she recovered quickly and
she joked, "Well I'm just everybody's cheerful bar-
tender." She hated herself for it, and swore that she
would tell him about it later, but she didn't.

MELANIE: *Many women believe that some men want their
woman to be a housekeeper or maid in their home, and not a
wife. They don't seem to be happy unless she's doing some-*

thing for him.

> IF A MAN OFFERS TO HELP ME WITH WORK INSIDE OF THE HOME, THIS SHOWS ME THAT HE UNDERSTANDS AND APPRECIATES MY EFFORTS.

The male world has its own natural order to it that most women can never comprehend. Men use words, terms, signs, gestures and codes that discourage most women from entering. Equally puzzling to many women is the way men are driven.

Take the week-end follies. Every Saturday and Sunday, men fill up the football and soccer fields, baseball diamonds, gyms, racquetball courts and weight rooms throughout America. Many of these men are either approaching or well-into their middle age. They play at boy's games, remembering times long past when they were young, fast and strong. The thought that they have lost their youthful edge (and physique) is too traumatic for many.

How do I know? Because each Saturday I would go to the local gym to play basketball. At the time, we only had one car, so my wife would drop me off on her way to do the grocery shopping. It never occurred to me that maybe she might want to watch the games or to play, too. That was wasn't part of the natural order of things.

ANDREA: *He likes to go to the football games and the race track with his friends. I don't have any idea what they talk about or do when they're together. And I don't ask. That's what he enjoys doing. I don't feel that I'm missing out on something or being left out.*

Unfortunately, when many of us think of drugs, gangs and high school drop-outs we think of black boys. When many of us think of prison, we think of black men. True, much of this thinking is a product of media-induced negative stereotyping, but, the problems are still real and troubling. Keeping their sons from falling victim to the gauntlet of American problems has become a full time job for many black women who must raise their sons alone. Some, in quiet ways, some, in forceful ways, serve as models of excellence for their sons.

ANDREA: *I don't see why women can't be role models for men. If he's into drugs or hanging around with pimps, then she should recognize the dangers and show by her actions that she doesn't approve or condone it. She should work positively to change the environment they live in and not give in to it.*

PUNK, SISSY FAGGOTT. If you want to start a fight, call a black man these names. Why have these words become so loaded? Could it be that these terms imply that men are like women? In the macho, hypercool, super-hip life style that many black men still desperately embrace, if a man is like a woman, he must be weak, scared and ineffectual. Real men, of course, aren't that way. They are: strong, courageous and effectual.

Many men protest and say that this is not the way they see women. Some are telling the truth. But, women continue to hear men call each other these names and they suspect that these terms may still mean more than men care to admit.

MELANIE: *One of the things I appreciate most about my husband is the way he often talks to me. I like the sweet tone in his voice when he asks me to do something or even calls my name. I think most women like to hear men talk like that.*

Remember in school when girls took home economics, cooking and typing, while boys took drafting, wood and metal shop? Remember when boys tried out for football, basketball, and track; and girls tried out for cheerleaders, yell queens and the drill team?

It was accepted then. If a girl wanted to take woodshop or drafting, she would have been discouraged. She might be asked how many carpenters or draftsmen she knew who were women? If she wanted to try out for basketball or track, she might be told that it was too dangerous. She could be injured, and besides, girls weren't supposed to sweat. Few girls made an issue of it then. Boys and girls knew that girls were being groomed for their assigned roles as housewives and homemakers.

Today, the prohibitions on classes and sports that girls can take have been tossed aside. But does participation mean parity? Tokenism is not just a word that applies when corporations and colleges let a few blacks through their doors. It can also apply to women who are bumping hard against the male-constructed glass ceiling in the business and professional world.

CARLA: *I know that there are some activities that are supposed to be a "man's thing," like working on cars. But there are a lot of men that don't know or care anything about cars and there are plenty of women who do. So I don't see anything wrong with the wife putting on some overalls and tinkering with the car if that's what she's good at and she likes doing.*

Bursting the Glass Ceiling

A REAL JOB! My mother was ecstatic when she announced that she had gotten a job at an insurance company. After years of cooking, cleaning and taking care of us, she was going to be a "real" worker. It meant so much to her.

When the day came to start work, she beat my father out the door. She rushed to the bus stop carrying a small brown paper sack containing her lunch.

The first few weeks on the job her, enthusiasm

remained high. She didn't wait for my father to ask her about her day. She excitedly described to him in minute detail everything that happened to her on the job that day. My father usually listened in silence.

This went on for a few months. After that, I noticed that my mother would say less and less about the job. I thought it was because of my father. I could sense that he didn't really like the idea of her working, but, he knew there was nothing he could do to discourage her once she had made up her mind.

He knew that working meant a great deal to her. And I'm sure he was not going to turn down the extra dollars that she would bring in. But my mother's silence made me curious. Why didn't she talk about her job anymore to me or my father?

CARLA: *Women still prefer to talk about their problems with other women. They don't feel comfortable telling men their intimate thoughts or feelings.*

It took nearly twenty years before I found out the truth. One evening I was looking through an old scrapbook when I found two letters. The first was written by my mother to the president of the insurance company where she worked. She complained about racial discrimination inside the company. The second letter was the president's reply. He denied that the company discriminated. I could understand how that deeply affected my mother. Still, I wondered if she had discussed her discontent with my father? If she didn't or felt she couldn't talk to him, it may be because there are times when men and women speak a different language, or have feelings that are incomprehensible to the other.

CARLA: *I think it's because women don't think men will be as responsive or sympathetic to them and they don't want to be rejected by them.*

In the United States, there are a mountain of laws that prohibit sex discrimination in the workplace. Take a brief stroll through any hospital, restaurant, elementary school, dental office, or government or corporate office, and you may wonder how much these laws have made a difference to women. More than 275 of the 504 occupations listed in the 1980 Census were filled mostly by women.

By 1990, the figures had improved—but not much.

Let's look even closer. African-American women filled the positions that paid the least and had the fewest benefits. If black men are only a notch above them on the income and occupation ladder, it means that troubled relationships will continue to be spelled MONEY.

ANDREA: *We had a problem once with the phone. I forgot to pay the bill and the phone was disconnected. He blamed me for it. To make sure that it didn't happen again, I put all the bills that needed to be paid right away in one pile and reminded him a week or so ahead of time that they're due. This way we knew that we had to put a certain amount of money aside to pay the bills.*

"It's a man's world." At least that's what soul singer James Brown declared in a popular hit song of the 1960s. Most black women didn't need to hear those lyrics to know that. Every off-color sexist joke in an office or factory tells them that. Every country club, corporate boardroom and craft union that excludes women tells them that. Many job or promotion rejections tell them that. The maze of rules and regulations that deny or reduce their welfare benefits tells them that. But women also remind men of the other line in James Brown's song: "It wouldn't be nothing without a woman."

ROSETTA: *I've worked in management at a couple of big companies and I got fed up playing the little games that you have to play to get ahead. No matter how hard you work or how well you play the game, they still don't take you seriously or appreciate you. I can tell by the way they talked to me and the type of work they gave me. It was always different than what they gave white men.*

Is the glass of progress half empty or half full for black women? While it's important to tell black women that they have "come a long way baby," black women are painfully aware that there's another side. They know that their poverty rate is higher than black men, and their income is less than white women.

No matter how many degrees, or how skilled the professional black women may be, they know that they are still perched on a precarious economic ledge. One push or shove from those who make the decisions in a hostile and unrelenting business and professional world can send them tumbling down. They are frustrated when they see black men and white women with the same educational and professional credentials as themselves attaining the American dream. Black women know that they are equally or more qualified than them.

Their tenuous economic position in American society often intrudes into their personal lives and creates tensions, self-doubts and anger in the home. The biggest casualty is their relationship with their men.

CARMEN: *We know our limitations financially and we try to work within them. If we have to spend more than we have budgeted for, we discuss it to see if we really need it. Most times, people spend and spend, and then hope they have enough money when the bills come due. Usually they don't and that's when the trouble can start in the home.*

During the past decade, black women have climbed higher than anybody else in the professions, mostly because they started so much lower than anybody else.

But progress is progress, and more black women have degrees, skills and income than ever. But they would be the first to tell you that they have not broken through the Ebony glass ceiling. Nor, are they any closer to erasing all the invisible signs that read: "For Men Only."

While they struggle for personal achievement and self-realization in the male-dominated business and professional world, they still must keep a household, raise children AND maintain their relationship with their men. This may be their biggest challenge of all.

> I CAN TELL BY THE WAY MEN WHO RUN THE COMPANIES TALK TO WOMEN THAT THEY DON'T TAKE THEM SERIOUSLY OR APPRECIATE THEIR WORK.

5

TILL DEATH DO US PART?

"I'm going to leave your father." It was just like my mother to skip the preliminaries and get right to it. She didn't even give me a chance to be surprised. Then she said, "I just want to be alone for awhile."

I knew that they had their share of arguments and disputes during their many years together. Sometimes in the midst of a heated exchange, one of them would shout that they were leaving for good. When I was younger and I heard my father threaten to leave, I would get scared. I thought he meant it. As time passed and I learned that "I'm going to leave" is almost a ritual utterance with even the most loving couples. I stopped worrying. The proof was that both were still there.

This time there was a note in my mother's voice that told me this might be different. She might actually mean it. It would be easy to say that I was thinking of them and their future. In reality, all I could think of was myself. For a terrible moment, the vision of being a child in a motherless home passed before my eyes.

It would be like the death of a loved one. I thought of the days and nights I would spend without my mother. Her voice, her face and her love were all gone. I panicked and blurted out, "but what will I do."

Each day, I watched and listened for a sign, any sign, that things had gotten better between them. A week, then two weeks went by. She was still there. I don't know what happened, maybe my father had sensed her resolve to leave and made some concessions that cooled her anger. Then, maybe my mother stood at the edge of the abyss of their marriage, looked down, remembering the good times they had in their long years together and shuddered at taking the frightful step past the precipice.

CARMEN: Th*e biggest problem between black men and black women is that they don't know how to talk to each other.*

What's the Hassle?

Fifty years ago, one in four blacks divorced. Today,

one in two blacks divorce. African-Americans are nearly three times more likely than whites to divorce, and ten times more likely than whites to separate. When they do break-up, they will leave more than one in three black children living in poverty. This could help sustain the dangerous spiral of crime, drugs, gangs and violence among young African-Americans. Worse, they will further weaken the fragile bond of trust between black men and women.

Still, African-Americans do marry. And nearly all black women who divorce recite a long trail of hurts, pains and indignities that seem like perfectly good reasons to them to end their relationships. But, there are women who walk down that same trail and don't leave. It comes down to how badly they want their marriage to work and how successful they are in getting their men to want the same.

CARLA: *Despite what people say, I think it's easy to leave when problems come up that you don't want to deal with. But I think in those times you need to pause for a moment, take a deep breath, close your eyes and try to visualize the good times you had together and the things that you did to get over problems in the past. Then you won't feel that you are trapped or that the situation is hopeless.*

Every couple has probably been told that two intelligent people can always work out their marital problems. The advice is as well-meaning as it is useless. If it was left to logic or intelligence there would be few wars, little hunger, no exploitation, racial, religious or sexual hatreds. The world would be a model of harmony, peace and order.

Individuals, however, don't live their lives purely on logic and intelligence. They have feelings, emotions and prejudices. Whether they are rational or irrational, they belong to that individual. People's heads are often clouded by their hearts. Only when they can put aside their feelings and see that others have feelings too, do they become the logical thinking persons who are capable of making the compromises and concessions that must strengthen relationships.

MELANIE: *A lot of men seem to have a real problem when women express anger at them. They get defensive. They feel that only a man has the "right" to get angry. But women are only expressing their feelings or frustrations. It doesn't mean that they disrespect the man.*

A few years ago, it was unheard of. Now, it has become a key part of some marriages. It's the marriage contract. At first, I thought it was something that wealthy people used to eliminate squabbles over money and property when they divorced.

I didn't realize that blacks were doing the same until one day I jokingly mentioned marriage contracts to a friend. He told me that he and his wife had drawn one up. I didn't think that he was a rich man and wondered why? What were they so paranoid about that they couldn't trust each other? Had marriage become so formalized that everything now had to be put in writing?

Maybe he read my thoughts. He quickly said that money and property were not the only reasons for their contract. They also included several items that specified their share of household duties and child care.

I thought about this for a long while. I still felt that love and devotion should be enough to overcome any misunderstandings. Then again, isn't marriage supposed to be a contract anyway?

ROSETTA: *If there's a problem, I don't think it helps to make threats, issue demands or give ultimatums. You should lay out the things that you'll work together on, set a time to discuss the issue or problem again, but don't let too much time pass.*

I want him to know that I want us to work together to solve the problem. This way I feel we can come to an agreement that we both feel good about.

Nearly a half century ago, millions of Americans laughed at the comic antics of Amos and Andy, first on radio and later on TV. For many Americans, the show confirmed and reinforced the images of buffoonery and ignorance that they had become accustomed to seeing in blacks. It took more than two decades of protest by the NAACP to get the series permanently removed from TV. But, the damage had been done. Many of the stereotypes had taken firm hold and would take more years to shake.

There was one image in particular that has had an enduring life, SAPPHIRE. She was the wife of one of the principal characters. In each show, Sapphire would run her household with an iron fist. She was loud, bossy and tough as nails. She constantly lorded her authority over her cowardly, conniving husband.

The Sapphire image was not new. It conformed to the carefully cultivated racist image of black women as domineering shrews who reduce their men to whimpering eunuchs. Composer W.C. Handy immortalized that image in a line in his famed *St. Louis Blues*: She "pulls dat man roun' by her apron strings."

Black women were enraged at the stereotype. But the image stuck. It is still the rare black woman that isn't called Sapphire at one time or another. The difference is that the ones who often call her that are black men. Sapphire has become a code word for men who want to avoid being "pressured" or given a hard time by black women.

Sapphire can also be a convenient cover for those black men who don't want to accept responsibility or make a full commitment to a relationship. Many black women insist that the only place Sapphire exists is in men's minds, not in men's lives.

CARLA: *It seems that when women ask men, "What do you want?" or "What can I do to improve the situation?" They misread it. They think that she is nagging or complaining. When she is just showing interest and concern.*

> DESPITE WHAT PEOPLE SAY, I THINK IT'S EASY FOR A MAN OR A WOMAN TO WALK-OUT RATHER THAN FACE PROBLEMS.

Taking Back Our Bodies I

It gave my friends and I great delight to spend countless hours trading boasts and swapping lies about our sexual conquests. We were engaging in more than just the standard ritual of male bonding. Our mostly fraudulent claims of sexual prowess gave us a feeling of self-esteem and identity.

If black women had to be trashed, belittled and, yes, victimized in the process, it was a small price to pay for securing our manhood. But maybe I shouldn't say that, because, in those days we didn't think of this as a price at all. It was a privilege to be men and in a position to say those things about "our women."

ANDREA: *A lot of men buy into the myth that they have to have sex, that they always have to have different women and that they can't control themselves or their urges. If women don't feel that they have to chase after sex, then men should feel the same.*

The code of silence on sex that many African-Americans embrace has stood up for decades. Many black men deny that they commit sexual abuses, victimize or mistreat their women. Some say that such charges are made mostly by feminists to further divide black men and women. Others say that such talk panders to racist stereotypes about "bad black men."

Lately, more and more women are breaking the code. This is why. The chances of a black woman being raped are ten times greater than a white woman. The chances of her being a homicide victim are four times greater. In nearly every case, her assailant is a black man. It is small consolation to her to say that most white women will be assaulted or killed by white men. Sexual abuse will remain an issue among African-Americans so long as the next potential victim is a wife or a lover.

MELANIE: *When a woman is abused, there are a couple of things she has to do. First, she has to get him to stop the physical abuse. She should talk to his mother, father or a close relative and try to get them to talk with him. They have to try and make him see the danger to himself and her. Next, she should try to establish a support system with close friends. The moment the abuse starts she has someone to turn to for help. They can offer her and the children a place to stay and run interference for her with him.*

Psychologists call it transference. The courts call it assault. African-Americans call it a tragedy. Whatever it's called, many black women are abused by their men. Often black men can't strike back at the oppressive conditions. So they take their frustrations out on those closest to them, their wives, lovers and children.

Dr. Martin Luther King, Jr. recognized that oppression, exploitation and abuse do not just come with a white face. He worried about it, so he tried to put it in the context of American oppression. His words are worth remembering:

Men unable to contain the emotional storms struck out at those who would be least likely to destroy them. They beat their wives and their children in order to protest a social injustice. The tragedy was that none of them understood why the violence exploded.

CARMEN: *A lot of men are either scared to express their feelings or don't have the verbal skills to say what's bothering them. They feel awkward, so pressure builds inside them and they strike out. He probably won't stop his abuse unless he can get in touch with his feelings and learn to talk out his problems rather, than using his woman as a punching bag.*

For many African-Americans, it was like being nailed with a right cross after being wobbled by a sharp upper cut. Less than a year after Anita Hill pointed accusing fingers at Clarence Thomas for sexual harassment, another black man and black woman were doing the same.

Former heavyweight champ, Mike Tyson was charged with raping a Miss Black America beauty contestant. The trial forced many blacks to choose sides. Many black men grumbled loudly that Tyson was a "scapegoat." They called the trial "racist." When Tyson was convicted and sentenced to prison they called it unwarranted.

Many black women saw it differently. They conceded that though his accuser was probably not blameless, the sentence was harsh. They would have preferred that Tyson receive counseling and make restitution. They also agreed that there was a racial double standard in the trial. More black men are tried, convicted and sentenced to longer prison terms for rape, than white men. And how many times they asked had white men been arrested for raping black women?

Still, they believed that Tyson was guilty and should be punished. They believed it because many of them could tell of their own experiences with black men who acted or tried to act the way Tyson did.

CARLA: *I'm convinced that most men don't see rape the same way women do. They think that a woman can't or shouldn't refuse to have sex with a man if she knows him, and maybe has dated him, or even has had sex with him before. And, if she does refuse and he forces himself on her, that couldn't be rape. They figure that she probably was just*

playing hard to get or that this is part of some game that
women play. But women know better.

I can understand why many black men find it
painful to admit that they do commit sexual abuses or
victimize women. Many whites still believe that black
men are sex charged studs who brutalize black women
and lust after white women. The myth has a long
history. It began with the European conquest in Africa,
gained credence during slavery, and was popularized
by writers, academics, novelists and the press during
the segregation era.

The myth of the black rapist and the loose black
woman were two sides of the same racist coin that was
used to deny black men and women justice and freedom. This twisted history also cost black men their
lives. Many were lynched, burned and shot in the
South on the charge that they made advances to white
women. Of the 455 men executed for rape, 405 were
black. Many whites came to believe that rape was a
"black crime."

After we clear away the falsehoods of the past, we
still must confront the realities of the present.

CARLA: *I try to use an analogy that a man can understand.*
I asked one man, suppose you are on a football or basketball
team and one of your teammates that you depended on, on the
field or the court, wanted to be your friend. He kept pestering
and approaching you, but you didn't want to be his friend.

Would you agree to be his friend because he was your teammate? A man knows that he wouldn't take it and he would tell him where to go fast.

For most men, the film *Fatal Attraction*, in which a woman obsessively harassed her male lover, was just a movie fantasy. Yet for many women the scenes rang true except they were the ones being harassed by men. More than a few can tell of their harrowing experiences after breaking off a relationship. I can relate to what they say. I found myself entangled in a male fatal attraction-type scenario involving my daughter.

After more than a year of dating Peter, my daughter decided to end her relationship with him. Even though she made it clear that she didn't want to see him, Peter continued to call her at home and demanded to see her. Finally, the problem came out. She tearfully told me that one day Peter showed up at one of her college classes and sat in the back of the room.

The next day, I went up to the campus with her. I notified the campus police of the problem. At the appointed class hour, accompanied by an officer, I went to the class to confront him. He was there. When the class ended the campus police promptly hustled him away, interrogated him and warned him not to return. The same day, we went to the local courthouse and applied for a restraining order to prevent him from further harassing her. Even when her "no" meant "no," Peter couldn't accept it. His ego got in the way of reality. He was a victim of himself, but so was my daughter.

IF WOMEN DON'T FEEL THEY HAVE TO CHASE AFTER SEX, MEN SHOULD FEEL THE SAME.

ROSETTA: *I've known men who were just friends. We've gone places together, and we've visited each other's apartments. There was no sexual attraction or interest involved. If a man and a woman have common interests they can be friends without feeling that they have to go to bed.*

More and more African-Americans attack the "white man's justice system." But like the situation with Peter, far too many personal feuds and disputes between African-American men and women still wind up in "the white man's court."

Many black women have no other choice. They know that the courts often don't take their complaints of neglect or abuse by black men seriously. The dilemma for African-American women is to find a way to communicate, either through face-to-face discussion or counseling, with their men before it goes to the "white man's court." That is the dilemma.

MELANIE: *If she has tried talking to him and that hasn't*

worked. If she has suggested therapy or counseling and he has refused to go. If he won't listen to a friend or a relative and the physical abuse is so severe that her life is at risk, then she has no choice but to turn either to the police or the courts. The danger is just too great for her to stay in the house with him.

Taking Back Our Bodies II

She sat quietly behind him, barely noticeable in the hot glare of the TV cameras and the popping flashes from the photographer's cameras. Cookie Johnson watched intently as the reporters peppered her husband, Magic Johnson, with questions. Gracious and smiling as always, Magic told the world that he had tested positive for HIV and was retiring from basketball.

For Cookie, there were few smiles. She would have to bear the twin burden of knowing that Magic could develop AIDS and that she could be infected too. And, since she was pregnant, there was the danger that their baby might be infected as well. Fortunately, neither has yet happened. She knew the risks to her body. And there would always be doubts and uncertainty. But she had made her decision. She would stand by him.

Earvin told me he'd understand if I wanted to leave. I couldn't believe it. I smacked him lightly on the face. 'Are you crazy?' I said. 'Why do you think I married you? I married you because I love you!

ANDREA: *A woman should try to make herself interesting.*
She should try to keep herself up physically and not run
around the house in old robes and hair curlers. She should
read and keep up on the issues. She shouldn't just talk to her
husband about bills or the problems with the kids or the job.
This way her man will be more likely to stay interested in her
and want to be with her, instead of out chasing other women.

The figures are staggering. Nearly half of all AIDS
victims are black. Of these, a growing number are
women and children. These are black men and women
who have contracted AIDS and have had unsafe sex or
have shared dirty hypodermic needles. It is a time for
deep soul-searching for many black men and women.
They look at each other and wonder if they or their
children could be the next victim.

CARLA: *A couple should be open and honest about sex.*
They should tell each other what they like and don't like.
Women often are afraid to tell men what makes them feel
good or what turns them off. They think that he might be
offended and withdraw. Most times he won't.

Other women aren't so sure that many black men
are capable of being open and honest about sex. One
woman told me:
A lot of women are scared to tell their boy friends what
their sexual preferences are. They think that he might think
that she's been fooling around with someone else or that she's

trying to make demands on him. They are really terrified that they might lose him, and a lot of times they are right.

Conspiracy? Plot? Genocide? These are terms that many African-Americans throw around. They are convinced that AIDS and the host of other diseases that infect them are the latest weapons used by "white America" to destroy African-Americans. Whether the new epidemic is coincidence or a plot is less important to many black women than the demand for sexual accountability by their men. Without that the consequences could be even more deadly.

ROSETTA: *Women have to protect themselves. If they are not into abstinence then they need to make sure they keep condoms around. And even then, they shouldn't feel guilty or ashamed to keep reminding men of the health risks from AIDS and other diseases.*

> A COUPLE SHOULD BE OPEN AND HONEST ABOUT SEX. THEY SHOULD TELL EACH OTHER WHAT THEY LIKE AND DON'T LIKE.

The fear and confusion that often reign among black women on matters of sex, health and their relationships are replaced by anger and emotion when the topic is abortion. In fact, the views of many black women on abortion are at odds with the prevailing notion among liberal political groups. They believe that black women enthusiastically endorse the pro-choice position.

But when blacks and whites were asked if they thought that abortion should be "always illegal," nearly twice as many blacks answered "yes" than answered "no." When asked whether they thought abortion should be "always legal," fewer than half the number of blacks than whites answered "yes." How could that be, after all, don't black women have just as much to lose as other women if abortion is outlawed? Aren't they the ones who also lack the funds to have abortions and access to the clinics that provide them? Like many other women, aren't they also the ones who also suffer injuries and death through botched "back alley" abortions?

With the dwindling numbers of black men unavailable to black women to choose from due to losses through death, divorce and desertion, can blacks afford to bring more children into fatherless homes, knowing that more than half of these homes will be poorer and needier? Perhaps. Many black women even without men are prepared to make the sacrifices. Some bow to peer pressure. Some believe in the sacredness of the family. Some simply want a baby to love. It's their choice.

ANDREA: *I am pro-choice. I don't believe you should bring*

kids into the world if you aren't ready to take responsibility for their welfare or don't have the financial means to support them.

ROSETTA: *I'm against abortion. No matter whether a woman is single or with someone, if they create a baby, it's a wonderful, even spiritual thing. That shouldn't be tampered with.*

More than once, I heard my mother say that she cried for nine months when she was pregnant with me. I didn't understand what she was talking about. Was there some health problem she had, or that I had that I didn't know about? Years later, I found out why she cried. She admitted that she didn't want me. She already had a son and a daughter. Those were all the children that she wanted or planned to have. I had upset the equation.

In those days when abortion was illegal, she had three recourses. She could try a self-induced abortion. This carried serious bodily risks. She could pay someone to perform a "back alley" abortion. This carried risks and was also costly. She could have the baby. Since my father wanted it, she was trapped by his wishes and the times. So she cried.

CARLA: *I agree that women have the right to an abortion. But, it wouldn't be right for me. If I got pregnant, I would hope that I had a good relationship with someone and we could work together as a unit to take care of our child. If I was single, I would try to make the necessary adjustments. I would try and increase my skills, education and certainly income to take care of my child.*

Good-bye Isn't Good Riddance

Many men have heard these words from their women, "Baby I don't think we can make it anymore." The words may sting. They tear at his guts. They weave layers of self-doubt about his manhood. They may jab at the deep fear of failure that haunt many men. While the break-up may mean broken dreams, it doesn't have to mean broken homes. It may present fresh opportunities for men to reassess their lives and learn from their mistakes. And, perhaps, they won't stumble over the same rocks.

CARMEN: *When a couple breaks-up, that's the time to step back, see what you did wrong, identify the problems or shortcomings. You probably should talk with someone who can be objective about you. Then you should take the steps to try to improve yourself.*

It's true that more men are taking responsibility for the care, nurturing and education of their children. There is a noticeable increase in the number of single parent homes where the single parent is not the mother but the father. Yet the numbers remain small. The real truth is that most children in broken homes will live with their mothers. For black teen girls, pregnancy continues to trap one in fourteen.

Even when these men don't marry the mothers of their children, they still can be a strong influence in the lives of their children. There is evidence many are. Despite what many believe, black men don't completely turn their backs on their children. Most absentee black fathers do acknowledge that the children belong to them. They visit occasionally and leave money, food or clothes. The goal is to encourage these fathers to do even more.

CARLA: *Most women want a man to be consistent with their children. If he says that he's going to call or come by on Friday to pick them up, he should. If he, says he is going to buy them a new coat or shoes, he should. If he says that he is going to talk to a teacher, he should keep the appointment and not expect you to keep it.*

While it's nice to say that absentee fathers should give more of their time and themselves to their children, the reality is that this doesn't pay the bills, money does. Many women aren't getting it from their men. Seven out of ten men paid either a token payment or nothing, and these were the men ordered by a court to pay. As one mother told me, collecting money from these men after a judgment against them practically takes an act of divine intervention.

Even this doesn't tell the real story. Less than three out of ten of the women who are awarded child support are black. With or without the courts, what are they to do?

MELANIE: *When I separated from my daughter's father, she told me that she wanted to live with him. At first he was reluctant, but after we both talked to him, and worked on him, he agreed. I packed her clothes and took her to his house. After all, it's not written in stone that a child has to live with her mother.*

I remember the conversation vividly. We stood in the kitchen of my father's small apartment. I had just broken the news to him that my wife and I were going to separate. He listened attentively as I poured out my agony. He could see my hurt. It was not easy to admit that after more than ten years of marriage you had failed, and had reached the end.

When I finished, my father said softly, "what about the children?" I didn't have an answer. My first thought was that I would leave my home and get an apartment ALONE. After all, wasn't that what men usually did when they separated?

When I mentioned that to him, he frowned and said, "Don't leave them." I was in a quandary. My son and daughter were still very young. When I meekly protested that I couldn't take care of them, he said firmly, "They are your responsibility." He would not listen to any excuses. No matter how bad a shape my relationship was in, to him children always came first. He was not going to let me forget that.

Fortunately, my wife agreed that children need both parents. Without any court involvement, we worked out a schedule to make sure that they spent equal time with each of us.

ROSETTA: *I was twenty-three when my real father called me for the first time. I hadn't seen or heard from him in years. I didn't know what to say to him and he didn't know what to say to me. I wanted to scream at him, "Where were you all these years?"*

MOST WOMEN WANT A MAN TO BE CON-SISTENT WITH THEIR CHILDREN.

After they break-up, most men and women want the burden of proof taken off of them. They want to pick up the pieces and move on. They realize that when they draw battlelines with each other, it quickly becomes a contest for children and money. On that battlefield, there are no winners, only victims.

ANDREA: *Some people can't or shouldn't be together. If you know that you're in a bad relationship, then you should put it behind you and move on.*

When I left the radio studio after finishing an interview on male parenting, a young man approached me and introduced himself. He said that he was a father, too, and that he was going through a very stressful battle with his ex-wife over their children. For three years, he had fought in the courts to gain joint custody of their children.

He said that he hadn't wanted to take her to court, but he felt she had pushed him to the wall. She refused to let him visit them or, talk to them on the phone and had returned his letters.

He was terribly bitter and frustrated over the shabby treatment. He felt that he had done everything a "good" father should do. He had sent money faithfully and had even offered to pay for a private school for the children. Finally, he stopped sending money hoping that this might make her come to her senses.

He blamed women for forcing some men to stop supporting their children. "They don't allow them to play a meaningful part in their children's lives." He felt that some women used their children as hostages to punish their ex-husbands for the wrongs or hurt they experienced. I told him that the women that I talked to deny this. They do not want to "use" their children as hammers against their fathers. They only want the fathers to pay their fair share.

He brushed this explanation aside. He was ready to fight back. He wanted to start a group of black fathers who were "wronged" by their ex-wives. Listening to him, I wondered how many women deliberately throw roadblocks into the paths of their men to keep them from their children, and then complained later that these men were "unfit fathers?" If men like him had done enough wrong to make some women feel that their children were better off without their fathers, what can fathers do to undo it?

CARLA: *If a man feels that he is being forced to do something by the court, a lot of times he becomes bitter toward his ex-wife. He takes it out on the woman through the children. He stops calling or visiting, and trys to think up some way to get out of paying child support.*

The Welfare Trap

They call it "Mothers Day." But, they are not referring to the warm day of remembrance on which Americans honor their mothers. "Mother's Day," for many black women, comes twice each month. On those days they pick up their AFDC welfare checks.

Drive by a check cashing stand on those days and you will see women standing in long lines waiting to cash (for a fee) their checks. Nearly half of the women who receive welfare payments are black. With the few hundred dollars they get, women are expected to feed and clothe themselves and their children, and pay rent. Their skill at stretching their meager welfare dollars would rival that of the manager of a money market fund. As one welfare recipient said, "anyone who can live on welfare should be courted by Wall Street."

Still, political conservatives love to take shots at the welfare system. They say it dulls initiative, diminishes the work ethic and discourages independence. Many black men and women agree. Some go further and rank welfare along with poverty, drugs, homicide and disease as a major destabilizer of the black family. Put bluntly, the maze of laws and regulations that reduce welfare benefits for families above certain income levels make it impossible for many black men to stay in the home and fulfill their role as responsible providers.

That's not all. Much of the media and many public officials turn the tables and make the woman the co-villain. They blame her for not being a "good mother," and claim that she is the reason many black teenagers join gangs, do drugs and commit violence. She can't win.

MELANIE: *I know many women who are on welfare and the father isn't making child support payments. They know where the father is and what he's doing. They don't report him because he gives them money every now and then, and spends a little time with the children. They go along with it because they want to maintain goodwill and keep up a relationship with him for the benefit of the children.*

What woman would say, "I don't need a husband.

I have the government to take care of me." Ridiculous? Of course, but, nearly half the states prohibit the "principal earner," almost always the husband, from receiving any welfare benefits. In the states that allow the "principal earner" to earn outside income, the amount is so low that they might as well not have a job.

Mercifully, most welfare agencies have stopped making late night closet and bedroom checks to see if a man is present. Now they simply run computer checks to see if the family has any added income. If they do, they deny or reduce their payments. This gives more ammunition to those who say that welfare puts the government in the business of family care, at the expense of gainfully employed husbands. If so, the system is a "poverty trap." A trap that is designed not to keep men in, but to keep them out.

MELANIE: *My oldest daughter's father promised to send money by a certain day. He didn't and he didn't call. I didn't call him and demand it then. I gave him two weeks. At the end of the two weeks, no money, no call. I told him that if he didn't have the money by the next day, we were coming to his house for dinner. If he wasn't there, we'd wait for him. He came up with the money because he knew it was his obligation and he didn't want the hassle.*

Toss out welfare? And then what? Without adequate education, and access to job and skill training programs, black men are caught in a bind. Without adequate child care, which for most poor black women is non-existent or prohibitively costly, black women are caught in a bind because they are unable to seek or hold a job. They are bound to a cycle of poverty and desertion that continues to destroy the black family. The binding must be unraveled.

ANDREA: *Just because you're poor doesn't mean that you can't improve your situation. You can try to learn a trade, take classes at night school, or hustle and find odd jobs or part-time jobs. I would do whatever it takes to lift myself up.*

Sexual victimization, violence, desertion, child maintenance, the right to choose versus the right to life. The problems seem overwhelming, but many black women are trying to cope. They recognize that America has put a special burden on black men. Yet they want their men to know that they are there to listen and support them, not to be a target of their abuse.

There is, however, a sad reality that confronts many black women and men. No matter how hard they try, their relationships may not work. When that happens, black men and women must be mature enough to recognize it and not take out their pain and frustrations on each other, or worse, make their children victims too.

The hope is that more men will become aware of

themselves as men and of the positive role that many women hold in their lives. Perhaps, in the future, when black men and women say good-by to each other, it does not have to mean good riddance.

6
A TALK WITH THEM

It's often said that black women raise their daughters and love their sons. When I hear that, I'm never sure whether this is said to flatter or put down women. I suspect that it's not meant as a compliment. The implication is that there is a double standard. Mothers demand that their daughters work hard, obey the rules and be responsible.

With boys it's different. Mothers pamper them, shelter them and make excuses for them. As men, they are spoiled and self-indulgent. Work is an afterthought, and, responsibility is something for others. Some black women accuse these men of always looking for their mother when they choose a mate.

If true, it would have disastrous consequences for black men. It would make shambles of their personal lives and relationships, create tension and hostilities in relationships with their women and children, and help perpetuate the cycle of poverty and destabilization within African-American communities.

Fortunately, that's not the memory I (and I hope other black men) have of the women who had a deeply profound influence on my life. For me, they were, my mother and my maternal grandmother.

Even though they have been dead nearly a quarter of a century, they are still a living presence in my life. On the special occasions, when my father goes to the cemetery to place flowers on my mother's gravesite, I don't go with him. It would be tantamount to admitting that she is dead.

I am not in a prolonged state of denial. I don't believe that she will be mystically reincarnated. And I am not wrapped up in maudlin sentimentalism. Both were tough, no-nonsense women. Even now when I am tempted to cut a few corners, my mother's words ring in my ear, "Things done by halves are never done right." Even now when I think of taking a step out of line, I can still feel the hard rap on my shoulder my grandmother would give me. I'm going to tell you about both of them.

First is my grandmother. Sociologist E. Franklin

Frazier called our grandmothers "the guardians of generations" and the "repository of folk wisdom." When he talked about our grandmothers, he must have had Althea Brown in mind. She didn't have much education. But, she always made sure that I read something every night. She would sit quietly while listening to me pronounce the words. If it didn't sound right, she would stop me and make me read it again and again and again, until she was satisfied that it sounded right.

Like many of our grandmothers, she lived and breathed God. She didn't care if people poked fun at her for being a Holy Roller. They could call this off-beat Pentecostal sect anything they wanted. But every Thursday night she and her grandson would faithfully attend the special healing services that were held in the cavernous building near 47th Street on Chicago's South Side.

I watched men and women shake, scream and talk in those funny words. (Some claim they're called Holy Rollers because they roll on the floor when the spirit of the Holy Ghost gets inside them.) Then they would march in a single file line down to the big pool of dark, murky water, where a man dressed in a white robe would push their heads under the water. I never asked my grandmother any questions about what they were doing. I knew that if she wanted you to know something, she would tell you.

I never knew why. Maybe she grew restless or

maybe she grew tired. Maybe she grew disillusioned with life in Chicago. One day she announced that she was leaving. She was going to live with her brother in Quincy, Illinois. My world suddenly came crashing down. The day we took her to the train station was the saddest of my life. I felt abandoned. She knew it. Before she got on the train, she made my mother solemnly promise to let me come to spend the summers with her.

My mother kept her word. For the next few summers I would ride the Illinois Central train south to the small town that nestled on the eastern bank of the Mississippi River. Quincy prided itself on being the gateway to Mark Twain country. The train stopped in Hannibal, Missouri, Twain's birthplace. Quincy also had the distinction of being the site of the sixth Lincoln-Douglas debate in 1858. For a brief time, Quincy enjoyed a little commercial importance as a river port for goods shipped down the Mississippi. But that was a century earlier, and times had long since passed the town by.

In the days I spent there, Quincy had the lazy feel of a small Southern town. Although, there were no "colored" and "white only" signs on the buildings, Quincy lay next door to Missouri, a former slave state, and was just as segregated as Jackson, Mississippi.

Many blacks lived in the small shotgun houses tightly clustered on three blocks near the town center. In Quincy, blacks didn't swim in the city's only pool, they swam in the dangerous currents of the Mississippi. The river claimed more than a few black lives. Blacks worked as janitors, or, if they were really lucky, they ran a small grocery store, barber or beauty shop.

Everybody knew everybody in the "colored" section and on hot nights when the old folks sat rocking and fanning on their front porches the children played into the long hours. There was always plenty of cool lemonade and iced tea to go around. I loved those summers, but I didn't love my grandmother's rules. I could not leave the house until all the chores were done. She didn't care if it took me all day. I would have to wash, sweep, gather the vegetables and eggs and run errands. The job wasn't finished until she said it was.

I didn't know it then, but she was teaching me basic survival skills. Despite her lack of formal education, she intuitively grasped what many grandmothers that raised boys knew. America could be a brutal and hostile place for a black man. A place where a man could expect few favors and look for no handouts. To make it, he would have to be able to stand on his own two feet and take care of himself. She wisely understood that decision-making and independence were the major ingredients for success. Without them, a black man could quickly drift into the wasteland of self-pity and failure. Perhaps she had seen too many men who had strayed into that land never to return. She was determined that "her boy" would not suffer their fate.

My mother, Nina Brown, was married to my father for nearly forty years, until her death from cancer. She worked tirelessly to make our house a home, even when she couldn't be in the home and had to work. She made sure that my grandmother kept a close watch on me. She seemed to know all my tricks and was always one step ahead of me. When it came to housework, she played no gender favorites. My brother and sister had the same household duties, and, like my grandmother, the job wasn't done until she said so.

The time she spent in and out of hospitals, the many operations, and the many hours she spent taking treatments and in therapy seemed to heighten the sense of urgency she felt for her sons. She was keenly aware of the pitfalls that awaited African-American men and was determined that her sons would avoid them. She continued to pound away on me about the importance of family, responsibility and women.

Her cancer fight also seemed to improve the sometimes stormy relations between her and my father. Perhaps, in the depths of pain and suffering they renewed their bond. I remember the days he would drive her to the American Cancer Society where she worked as a volunteer. My father would wait for her while she spent hours talking with other patients and helping plan activities. I know that her illness had a profound effect on him. I think it made him more tolerant and supportive.

I remember the phone call from my father the day

she died. All he could say was, "she's gone, she's gone" as he sobbed uncontrollably. In that savage moment his tears told me how much she meant to him.

My mother and grandmother were modern women in an era when America refused to recognize the rights or dignity of women. Well into the 20th century, married women had virtually no legal rights, and were treated as near wards of their husbands. Some states even prohibited wives from owning property in her own name or filing lawsuits. As late as the early 1970s, several states still required that wives must live wherever her husband chose or be charged with abandonment. It took a Supreme Court ruling to strike this down.

They were proud black women in an era when America refused to recognize that neither black men or women had any rights that a white man was bound to respect. For nearly all their adult lives segregation, was the law of the land, while several hundred black men AND women were lynched yearly.

I can't physically talk with them as I did with my father in B*lack Fatherhood: The Guide to Male Parenting*. I can construct an interview with them based on comments and remarks I heard them make over the years, as well as with my remembrance of the conversations we had. I also will draw on the memory of my father and my knowledge of my family history. Like the other women in this book, I want them to tell us about their men. I believe that scattered among their recollections of yesterday's problems, may still rest a few of today's solutions.

Before we begin, let me tell you what makes their story even more remarkable. They did not have to live as black persons. Unlike most African-Americans, blackness did not mark them with an indelible stamp of inferiority from birth. Both were so fair skinned that they could have passed for white.

My grandmother was nearly a perfect blend of Caucasian and Choctaw Indian with only the barest trace of "black blood." My mother had green eyes, near white skin, and light brown straight hair. Yet at no time during their lives did they consider being anything other than black. By casting their lot with blacks, they knew they would pay a price. They caught it from both sides. Not only did they suffer segregation and the countless insults, slights and indignities from whites, they often heard themselves called "white bitches" by angry and frustrated blacks who mistook them for white. Through it all, they kept the faith. They trusted in the future, and they believed in their family. Now my mother and grandmother will talk to me and to each other about their men.

EH: What kind of man was your father?

Nina: *I didn't really know him that well. He left home when I was very young. Why he left I don't know. But I can tell you what kind of man I envisioned him to be.*

EH: How was that?

Nina: *He was his own man. He stood up for what he believed in and what he thought was right. He did not back away from difficult tasks because he was scared of failing. I say that because it seems in those days black men were tougher, and had more of a sense of identity. Remember there was no welfare, social security in those days, and most black men didn't have pensions, insurance or much of a savings to fall back on when a crisis came up. They knew they had to rely pretty much on their own resources and initiative. So they stuck close to their families and were pretty conscious about seeing to the needs of their wives and children as best as they could. If they had to leave for whatever reason, they made sure that their families had a place to live, oftentimes with one of their relatives. They almost always sent some money, food or clothes. They tried to be responsible men.*

Althea: *I won't say what happened between my husband and I. But during the time we were together, he took an active interest in his kids. And he was very strict. There were rules of the house that they had to adhere to. When he left, even though it was hard, I was able to keep the family together by doing washing, cleaning and anything else that would bring in some dollars. Sometimes that wasn't enough. He would send money and, although it wasn't much, it got us over the rough spots. Strength and independence are qualities that women had too.*

EH: How do you want a man to treat you?

Nina: *Most women would say that they want a man who is kind, considerate and respects them as a person. That's fine. But I don't think that's enough. I always wanted a man who would understand me. By that I mean recognize my need to be independent and the freedom to express myself the way I want. Maybe I expected too much. Men then were very traditional in their thinking. They expected women to conform to the standard roles. There were few men enlightened enough to allow their women to step out of those roles. Most of us willingly, some grudgingly, made our compromises. We performed our duties as cooks, cleaners, laundry maids, childbearers and rearers. We didn't complain, but many of us secretly dreamed of being free to become the type of person that we wanted and not the kind of person that men expected us to be.*

Althea: *I look at it a little differently. I think a man should naturally be the protector of the family. I always saw the relationship between a husband and a wife as a partnership. He worked and she worked. The only difference was that one was outside the home, the other was in the home. They both had the same goal, to provide for their family. So, if the wife did the cooking cleaning and child rearing. Was that bad?*

I think that's partly what's wrong today with our young people. It's not just the men, but the women, too, who aren't in the home taking care of business.

EH: So, you would want your man to make the important decisions?

Althea: *Yes. You can't have it both ways. If you want your man to truly be a man, you have to get behind him when he takes the initiative.*

Nina: *That's true, but being a man to me doesn't mean having someone control your life. I think there's a danger that if women let men make the major decisions, that can easily slip over into dominance. I think in a relationship based on trust and mutual respect, decisions should be made only after both parties have had their say.*

EH: Does that mean that men and women should share equally in the running of the home?

Nina: *Are you referring to household chores and taking care of the kids?*

EH: Yes.

Nina: *Yes and no. Yes, he should take part in the planning and organizing of the family activities. And that means taking responsibility for doing some housework when he's there. That's not asking too much, especially when I noticed that men have a lot of free time to sit and watch TV or go out with their friends.*

No, because in the case of your father, he worked hard,

put in long hours at the post office and always brought home
his pay. As long as he did that, I didn't get upset. I knew that
if he put the food on the table, the least I could do was cook
it. Like your grandmother said, in that situation, it was a
logical division of labor.

EH: But you wanted to work, too?

Nina: *Yes. I wanted to work and pursue my own career.
But then there were severe limits on what women could do.
Before World War II, the best most black women could hope
for was a job as a domestic, maid or some kind of service
worker. They didn't open the plant work to us until the war,
and then we got less pay than the men. For a while, I tried
work as a domestic, but I knew that wasn't for me. Later I
took a correspondence course, because I wanted to prepare
myself to be something more than just a housewife or a maid.
When I finally did get a better job, your father was forced to
do some things in the house, but even then it wasn't equal.
I still did most of the cooking and cleaning.*

IN THOSE DAYS BLACK MEN STUCK
CLOSER TO THEIR FAMILIES AND THEY
WERE PRETTY CONSCIENTIOUS ABOUT
SEEING TO THE NEEDS OF THEIR
CHILDREN.

Althea: *You and your husband were able to do both jobs.
It doesn't sound like either one of you suffered for being a*

worker and doing housework. It still gave you the chance to make sure your kids received the proper guidance.

EH: A major problem today is sexual abuse and domestic violence. Most states have tough laws, at least on paper, against rape and sexual violence. But some states also have laws against spousal sexual abuse. I know those things weren't openly talked about, let alone legislated against back then....

Althea: *That's true, there were no laws then. Women were treated as pretty much an extension of their husbands, and most women didn't think much about that. But people, especially women, did talk about it among themselves. They knew who the men were who beat their wives and children. It was frowned on, and they were pointed at, stared at and shunned. It was a way of ostracizing them.*

We took care of it ourselves. The minister would go have a talk with the man and try to get him to see that what he was doing was wrong. If it got real bad and persisted, then the wife would take the kids and leave, go stay with relatives, parents or even close friends. It also wasn't unusual for her father or brothers to show up at the house to apply a little gentle pressure to stop what he was doing. It let him know that he was flirting with danger and that it could be dangerous to his health.

Nina: *I don't think it was quite the problem that it is today. A man might get drunk and hit his wife, but I don't* remember the wholesale violence and sexual abuse that we see today. Remember, people were closer, religion had a stronger hold on people, and values were different. For better or worse, men considered it their duty to protect women. In that sense, it worked in our favor. Also sex then was considered more of an obligation and responsibility, then for pleasure. So that also had its self-imposed limits.

EH: What about premarital sex and pregnancy?

Nina: It was a taboo subject, but people did have sex before marriage and women got pregnant. Then, a women could keep the baby. She could make sure that the man did the right thing and married her, even if it meant dogging his trail if he tried to leave town. Or she could have an abortion.

EH: An abortion, then?

Nina: Of course, just because it was illegal didn't mean that women didn't have them. It was risky, especially for black women, who didn't have the money or the access to someone who would do it. Many lost their lives trying to do it themselves. Also, many women had abortions who were married and had the means to take care of their children. They just decided they didn't want to have children or they didn't want any more children. It was a choice that they made.

EH: Did you believe that when two people said "till death do us part" it meant exactly that?

Nina: *In the beginning I did. And so did most other women. The way we were brought up, when we recited the marriage vows, it was forever. And even if some women didn't totally commit themselves to marriage, they stayed in the marriage because the divorce laws were very restrictive then. You had to prove adultery or desertion.*

Also, women valued their "reputation." The worst thing was to be thought of as a "loose woman." So people tried to make the best of what often were horrendous personal situations. And then there were the children. If a child didn't live with both parents, that was considered by most people to be a badge of shame.

Later, when I realized that life was too short and that I had certain goals that I wanted to achieve, I knew that I couldn't center everything around the home and children. There was a big world out there and I wanted to be a part of it. That's probably when the conflicts began.

EH: How did you deal with those conflicts?

Nina: *Through talk, but sometimes that wasn't enough. In those days, most men thought that they should have the final word on things and that certainly included your father. So there were times when I had to put my foot down and let him know that if he really loved and valued me, he would respect my wishes, too. I tried to do it in ways that I felt*

*wouldn't threaten him, or make him feel that I was picking
an argument for the sake of it. For instance, when I wanted
to go to work, I pointed out to him that the children were older
and could take care of themselves. I tried to show him that my
working wouldn't interfere with the household chores, and
that with the extra money we would be able to buy better
furniture and even build our savings. He grumbled about it
at first, but he could see that I was right.*

EH: It sounds like you took a more tactful approach?

Nina: *I did. I knew that was the only way that I could get
what I wanted and still keep the peace. I didn't feel that I was
compromising myself or being meek.*

Althea: *What she doesn't say is that she also had her
mother living with her to look after the house and the kids. I
was happy to do it, because I could see that she wanted to do
more with her life.*

EH: What happened when there were conflicts that
you couldn't resolve through talk?

Nina: *There were plenty of them. There were times when
I thought of leaving. In fact, once or twice I actually packed
my bags. But then he saw that I meant business, he would
usually make an overture or become more reasonable. Several times we talked to our pastor to try to resolve a conflict.
Fortunately, he was a good listener. He also had a lot of*

experience with couples.

After we told our side of the story, he would take us aside individually and try to get us to see the other's person's reasoning. This usually worked. I still might want to get my way, but at least I could understand why he was acting the way he did. I found that it helps to have someone you can talk to and get insight from.

It has to be someone who can see both sides and can be impartial. There's just too much emotionalism involved when a man and a woman bump heads. Things are usually said that neither one really means, but sometimes, once your mouth gets ahead of your head, you can do a lot of harm. And some time will have to pass before the bad feelings die down and things can return to normal.

EH: So, you were always able to work through your problems?

Nina: *Most of the time. But I want to add this. I don't think that two people should stay together just for the sake of staying together. There are situations where there's a long pattern of physical or mental abuse. Or the man may be having an affair, chasing women, not contributing anything to his wife or children, and is chronically absent from the home. Then if she has any self-respect she has to take action. That could mean separation or divorce. When that happens, she should go to court or do whatever it takes to make sure that he at least provides financial support for the children.*

I wouldn't stop there. He is still the father, and if he

shows that he genuinely wants to be involved with his children, I think she should try to make it as easy as possible for him to call, visit and spend time with the children. She shouldn't be threatened by this. It will help her in the long run, since boys and girls need to have a positive male presence in their lives. It will relieve her of the physical and emotional burden of dealing with her children alone.

Althea: *I disagree. I think marriage vows should be taken seriously. It takes a lot of love, dedication and commitment to make it work, but it can work. People have to stop being so selfish and always just thinking about what they want. If they have children, remember that there are other lives and feelings involved that have to be considered. Nowadays a man or a woman may want to run away the first time something comes up in their marriage that they think they can't deal with.*

If thoughtfulness and consideration are not enough to keep a couple together, then men should consider this. From what I hear, if you're married you'll live longer and have fewer health problems.

IN THE BEGINNING OF MY MARRIAGE I BELIEVED THAT IT WAS FOREVER. LATER, I REALIZED THAT I HAD CERTAIN GOALS I WANTED TO ACHIEVE. I KNEW I COULDN'T CENTER EVERYTHING AROUND THE HOME AND CHILDREN.

EH: You're right. African-American men die younger. They have more chronic health problems, suffer higher incidence of alcoholism and drug addiction, and their unemployment rates are double that of white males. All of this certainly works to disrupt the black family.

Nina: *When the black man suffers, the black woman suffers, too. If he is unemployed, his family is going to be poorer. If he is sick or in jail, she is going to have to carry the load of taking care of the family. If he feels frustrated and depressed, he, more than likely, is going to take it out on her.*

This is why black women have to be strong and supportive. She can encourage him to take classes, enroll in a training program to improve his job skills, and help him prepare resumes. If he has an alcohol or drug problem, instead of berating or condemning him, she can try to get him to get into a counseling or therapy program.

There are ways she can gently push her man without making him think that she's against him. That's important, because a lot of black men think that when their wives or girlfriends try to help them with a problem, they take it as criticism and accuse them of being against them. Most times it's not true. They want the best for them because they know inside that if he's not happy, they won't be happy either.

EH: Isn't that putting the burden on women?

Nina: *In a way, yes. Black women have always faced a double challenge. They've had to battle the prejudices of white society and the prejudices of their men. So, this has toughened us and given us the ability to see the broader picture. We have never been content to take a back seat to men. Women tend to be more social. We join organizations and we plan activities and affairs. We can use that talent to build and expand organizations such as the National Council of Negro Women, sororities, women's clubs, church groups and push for more programs to benefit black people.*

Althea: *Women are usually more patient and tolerant than men. They can effectively use those qualities to prevent or reduce conflicts and disputes in the home. Most men want to have their way and control situations. But a woman can select the issues that are important to her, and make her points without turning the situation into a confrontation or a power struggle with her man.*

EH: It sounds like you're also putting the burden on black women?

Althea: *No, I'm saying that society has done that by victimizing black men and denying them their manhood. So, women many times were forced to be more out front both inside and outside the home.*

EH: What do you say to those who say that black men must take the lead?

Nina: *I have mixed emotions. As I said before, I want a*

man to be strong and independent. I want him to stand up for what he believes. And I think most women would like to see their men take the initiative in fighting the big battles. Thankfully, throughout our history we have had men that have been strong role models in business, the professions, trades, organizations and with their families. That's fine. But when you say leadership, I think that you can't necessarily define it by sex alone. It requires talent, vision, thought and goals. Men don't automatically have those qualities just because they are men. Many women have those qualities. Sometimes black men will take the lead. Other times black women will lead. And there will be times when they both will

Althea: *I'm old fashioned. I still think that a man should be a man. To me that means that he should take the lead. Women have had to hold things together for a long time. Now it's his turn.*

EH: How did you manage to stay together for nearly forty years?

Nina: *I'll say it again. In the beginning, I felt I had an obligation to stay together. That's not to say that love didn't play a strong part in it. But marriage then was a duty that you didn't really question. Later, when the kids were older, and I wanted a career, it required new adjustments. It was a painful process. At any point, our marriage could have collapsed. Fortunately, both of us had the insight and maturity to make the little gestures and compromises. We learned* to give as well as take. We came to understand that compromise was not a dirty word. Once we got to that point, we felt better about ourselves and each other.

Let me give you an example. In 1954 we drove out to California. I fell in love with the place at first sight. Everything there seemed so fresh and new. I wanted to move there right then and there, but I knew that your father wasn't ready to retire from the post office yet. He liked his job. He had a lot of friends. He was a church trustee, a postal union representative. He belonged to the Shriners and the Elks. He played in the National Guard band. He was active in local politics. And we owned an apartment building.

I didn't make an issue of moving. I waited and kept dreaming about it. As it got closer to the day when he would retire, I began talking with him about it. I tried to get him to see the advantages, like the weather, lower living costs, and real estate opportunities. He finally gave in. It was rough the first few months. He really missed Chicago. But when winter came and he could sit outside on the porch in the sun, he came around and admitted that it was the right move.

I was willing to COMPROMISE and he was willing to CHANGE. That was our secret.

7
BRING HIM BACK HOME

The pastor was visibly moved by the story the young married couple had told him. Sid had just lost his well-paying job as a data processing technician at a major aerospace company. About the same time, Carol had gone on maternity leave from her job at an auto parts manufacturing company. Their debts piled up and they had fallen several months behind in their rent payments. Now they faced eviction.

Sid had become very irritable and morose. When Carol tried to talk with him about their problems, he would fly into a rage and storm out the house. Sid had begun to spend more time away from the home. Carol knew that their marriage was crumbling. It took some doing, but she got him to agree to go with her to see their pastor.

The pastor could see that Carol loved Sid, and he guessed that Sid didn't really want to leave her. He was especially impressed by Carol's resolve to hold their marriage together. Other than an occasional question about their finances, the pastor mostly let them talk.

He made them promise to come back several days later to talk with him again. The next time he would try to get them to take the next step and talk to each other. As they left he pressed some money into Sid's hand and told him to "consider it a loan."

The next week when they returned, Sid told him they had moved to a smaller place, and that he had found a temporary job. The couple did not kiss and fall into each other's arms and there would be no storybook ending to their dilemma. Carol knew that their marriage was in trouble. She was not going to sit and wait for Sid to make things right. Carol did what many other black women have done. She took action to bring her man back.

ANDREA: *I would try my best not to pressure him to live up to certain standards that probably aren't realistic.*

Dear President Roosevelt:

Why must our men fight and die for their country when it won't give them a job they are fitted for? They would rather fight and die for their families. My husband is young, intelligent and very depressed over this situation. We want to live, not merely exist from day to day, but to live as you or any human being desires to do. We want our unborn children to have an equal chance as the white.

I don't know whether President Franklin Roosevelt actually read the letter from Mrs. Henry Weddington or not. It was one of thousands that he received daily at the White House. But the elegant simplicity of her words carried a force and power that certainly would have moved the president. Mrs. Weddington, unemployed and ill, was forced to live on the twenty-six dollars a month that her husband earned working on the Depression-era Works Progress Administration government work program. Mrs. Weddington's letter captured the spirit of two people locked together in life's struggle for survival. It also showed the commitment of a black woman to her man.

CARMEN: *I try to let him know any way I can that I support him.*

- The number of black families headed by black women has tripled.

- One in two black families with children are headed by women.
- Black female-headed families make less than one third the national median income.
- The majority of children who live alone with their mothers are poor.

Saying these things may sound like a broken record, but if black men and women don't halt this, who will?

CARLA: *I would tell him that he has talents and skills, too. And I would encourage him to use them.*

A black man may lose a job or not be able to find one. He may be harassed by the police or jailed. They may be at risk from street violence. He may suffer a debilitating illness. Many black men turn to drugs, alcohol, tobacco or gambling to escape. They often refuse to recognize that they have a problem. But their women do. They watch in horror as their men slip deeper into the emotional depths. They have three choices: they can sink with them. They can leave. Or they can work hard to rescue their men from the depths.

ROSETTA: *If the problem is really serious, you have to detach yourself emotionally and play the part of a friend. If you continue to be the wife or girlfriend, you will suffer too, and this doesn't help him or you.*

> # I TRY TO LET HIM KNOW ANY WAY I CAN THAT I SUPPORT HIM.

In the twelve years they were married, they hadn't eaten together more than seven or eight times. He had committed many acts of sexual infidelity. He was indicted for cocaine use and sale. He was the subject of a barrage of media reports and stories, nearly all negative. He was convicted on the cocaine charge and served a prison sentence.

It would have been easy for Effie Barry to have called it quits and to leave Marion Barry. The Mayor of Washington, D.C., a drug addict and convicted trafficker, had certainly done enough to embarrass his wife and son. If she had chosen to leave him, many would have understood, and probably, even applauded her for her courage.

That wasn't what she had in mind. Even as her world came crashing down around her, she did not cry for herself but for him: "I was hurt, very saddened, I just felt so bad for him."

Was she a fool? Was she living a lie? Was she a martyr to the misguided actions of a troubled black man? Was she sacrificing herself for some mistaken notion of loyalty to family? Some might say that love must have limits or it becomes a perverse exercise in masochism or self-pity. Eventually, Effie would separate from Marion. It was not an easy decision for her to make. She had tried hard to trudge through her vast desert of sorrows to find the small oasis of hope to renew her marriage. That was the price she was willing to pay to bring her man back home.

MELANIE: *If he has a problem, so do you.*

I do not believe that black women want to emasculate black men. I do believe that more black women want to support and share their lives with their men. I do believe that many of the black women who attacked the character and worth of black men are now ready to have an open and honest relationship with black men.

But they also want to know that their men are willing to return that same love and trust. Commitment is not a shameful word nor a weakness. Commitment does not compromise manhood, it enhances it. The road is littered with the broken wrecks of men who have jumped from one woman to another trying to find nirvana. They have become disappointed, bitter and lonely.

CARMEN: *I've always believed that for a relationship to really work, it must be a partnership.*

An Ethiopian proverb says, "When spider webs unite, they can tie up a lion."

In *Black Fatherhood: The Guide to Male Parenting*, I said that black men may not be all that we want them to be. They are men with all the strengths and weaknesses of other men.

This is not a revelation to black women. Their men have taken them to the heights of fulfillment and plunged them to the recesses of despair. Their men have caused them joy and pain. Their men have brought them hope and disappointment. Through it all, black men remain the men with whom black women seek to unite their webs. As long as they do, they will continue to tie up the lion.

Appendix

Interview Questions

SOME QUESTIONS MAY NOT APPLY. PLEASE BE BRIEF AND SPECIFIC WITH THE ANSWERS TO THESE QUESTIONS. ALSO, THINK OF A SPECIFIC SITUATION OR CONVERSATION WITH YOUR HUSBAND/ SIGNIFICANT OTHER TO GO WITH YOUR ANSWER.

Introduction

Chapter 1 — The Father Mystique
- How did you view your father?
- What ways did your father provide comfort (and nurturing) for you?

Chapter 2 — Looking For "Mr. Right"
- What specifically do you (women) look for in a man?
- Should black women date/marry white men? How to prevent it?
- Should black men date/marry white women? How to prevent it?
- What compromises and sacrifices are you willing to make?
- How can a relationship be maintained and sustained when there is a shortage of black men?

Chapter 3 — Behind, Beside or In Front of Him?

- What kind of decisions should your man/a man make in the home or outside of it?
- What kind of decisions should you make and not leave to him?
- How do you support him when he makes a decision?
- The need to be dominant, how do you handle the "male ego"?
- Do you boost it? Should you boost it?
- How can/do you build a true partnership with your man?
- How can women help men to be more sensitive and caring?

Chapter 4 — I Work Hard Too!

- What should your man do to help you in the home?
- What can (activities) a father do to raise or help raise children?
- Are there things that he should do more of?
- Are there things that he shouldn't do at all?
- When both work, how do you handle money questions within the home?

Chapter 5 — Till Death Do Us Part?

- What steps do you take to resolve your conflicts?
- What ways can you protect yourself against sexual exploitation/ physical abuse?

- How can you keep conflicts out of the courts and away from the police?
- What should sexual accountability in men mean?
- How can men prevent the spread of AIDS? Other Sexually Caused diseases?
- When and why should black women use abortion as a means of birth control?
- How can a father truly be an equal partner in raising children when he's not in the home?
- How can money/support for children be gotten from him without resorting to courts?
- What can a woman on welfare do to keep her man from leaving?
- What should a man whose family is on welfare try to do to keep it together?

Chapter 7 — Bring Him Back Home
- What steps can you take to prevent him from leaving you? Or you from leaving him?
- How can you and him combat societal problems like alcohol, drugs, gambling, unemployment that may push him out of the him?
- What can you do to maintain warm relations with him when he has permanently left the home?

Optional
- Can a woman do anything to keep her husband/ significant other from going to prison/away from crime?

- If he's in prison can you/should you maintain a relationship? and how?

References

Introduction

Page

3   Andrew Billingsley, *Black Families in White America* (Englewood Cliffs, N.J.: Prentice-Hall, 1968), 40-48.

3   Sojourner Truth quoted in Toni Cade, *The Black Woman* (New York: Penguin Books, 1970), 92.

4   Quoted in Gerda Lerner, ed., *Black Women in White America* (New York: Random House, 1972), 48.

5   Quoted in Lerner, *Black Women in White America* , 216.

6   Alfreda M. Duster, ed., *Crusade for Justice: The Autobiography of Ida B. Wells* (Chicago: University of Chicago Press, 1970).

7   Quoted in Lerner, *Black Women in White America,* 228.

Chapter 1 — The Father Mystique

16 Murray, Pauli, *Song in a Weary Throat* (New York:

Harper & Row, 1987), 12.

17 Herbert G. Gutman, *The Black Family in Slavery and Freedom, 1750-1925* (New York: Random House, 1976), 45-100.

18 Goodard, Lawrence and Covill, William E. III, "Black Teenage Parenting," in Reginald L. Jones, ed., *Black Adolescents*, 373-383.

18 Andrew Billingsley, "Understanding African-American Family Diversity," in the National Urban League, *The State of Black America, 1990* (New York: NUL, 1990), 89-90.

18 Judith A. Seltzer shatters the myth that absentee black fathers do not maintain contact with their children or provide any financial support for them. See, "Relationships between Fathers and Children who Live Apart: The Father's Role After Separation" in *Journal of Marriage and the Family,* 53 (February, 1991), 94.

19 Moynihan, Daniel Patrick, *The Negro Family: The Case for National Action,* Washington: U.S. Government Printing Office, 1965), 30.

21 Pierre Grimal, ed.,*World Mythology* (New York:

Excaliber Books, 1981), 142.

24 Rubenstein, Ed, "How Many Homeless," (*National Review*, May 14, 1990), 17.

Chapter 2 — Looking for "Mr. Right"

30 Malcolm X with Alex Haley, *The Autobiography of Malcolm X* (New York: Grove Press, 1966), 234.

36 Eldridge Cleaver quoted in Toni Cade, ed., The *Black Woman* (New York: Penguin Publishers, 1970), 139.

39 Elizabeth Stone, "Love vs. Bigotry," in *Glamour Magazine*, February, 1992:168.

40 Laura B. Randolph, "Black Women-White Men: What's Goin' On?, *Ebony*, March, 1989:154-155.

46 The Harvard Study is cited in Lynn Norment, "What Black Women Really Want in a Man," *Ebony*, March, 1992:30.

47 "How Black Women Can Deal with the Black Male Shortage," Ebony, May 1986:9.

49 Eugene Hillman, *Polygamy Reconsidered: African*

Plural Marriage (Maryknoll, N.Y.: Orbis Books, 1975).

Chapter 3 — Behind, Beside, In Front of Him?

53 The author was in attendance at the speech given by Eldridge Cleaver in 1969 in Los Angeles.

54 Patricia Hill Collins, "The Meaning of Motherhood in Black Culture," in Robert Staple, ed., *The Black Family* (Belmont, CA.: Wadsworth Publishing Co., 1990), 169-178.

55 Lorraine Hansberry, *A Raisin in the Sun* (New York: New American Library, 1958), 23.

58 Joanne M. Martin and Elmer P. Martin, *The Helping Tradition in the Black Family* (Silver Spring, Md.: National Association of Social Workers, 1985), 20.

59 Frederick Douglass, *The Life and Times of Frederick Douglass* (New York: Collier Books, 1962), 143.

61 Robert Chrisman and Robert L. Allen, *Court of Appeal* (New York: Ballantine, 1992). Forty-four black activists and scholars debate the pros and cons of the Thomas-Hill clash.

62 *Malcolm X Speaks* (New York: Merit Publishers,

1965), 24.

68 Mafari Moore, Gwen Akua-Gilyard, Karen King and Nsenga Warfield-Coppock, detail the female rites of passage program in *Transformation* (New York: Stars Press, 1987), 25.

69 M.W. Taylor, *Harriet Tubman* (New Haven: Chelsea House Publishers, 1991), 50-51.

72 Richard Wright, *Uncle Tom's Children* (New York: Harper & Row, 1965), 4.

Chapter 4 — I Work Hard, Too!

77 Elizabeth Fox-Genovese, *Within the Plantation Household* (Chapel Hill, N.C.: University of North Carolina Press, 1988), 177.

78 Harvey Sitkoff, *A New Deal for Blacks* (New York: Oxford University Press, 1978), 321-323.

81 Educational Testing Service Report, "Number of Black Women in College on Steady Rise," *Jet Magazine*, June 24, 1991:24.

81 Claudette E. Bennett, *The Black Population in the United States, March 1989 and 1990,* Current Popula-

tion Reports Series P. 20, No. 448. (Washington, D.C.: Government Printing Office, 1991), 9-13.

81 Marilyn French, *The War Against Women* (New York: Summit Books, 1992), 185.

83 Barbara R. Bergman, *The Economic Emergence of Women* (New York: Basic Books, 1986), 317.

91 "Women: Law Doesn't Stop Discrimination," *Los Angeles Times*, August, 17, 1992:16.

Chapter 5 — Till Death Do Us Part?

97 Reynolds Farley and Suzanne M. Bianchi, "The Growing Racial Difference in Marriage and Family Patterns," in *The Black Family*, 7-8.

100 Daniel J. Leab, *From Sambo to Superspade* (Boston: Houghton-Mifflin Co., 1975), 98.

101 W.C. Handy quoted in E. Franklin Frazier, *The Negro Family in the United States* (Chicago: University of Chicago Press, 1966), 212.

103 Martin Luther King, Jr., Where Do We Go From here: Chaos or Community? (Boston: Beacon Press, 1968), 107.

104 The Mike Tyson case and black male victimization of black females is detailed in the *Guardian*, March 11, 1992:18.

104 Department of Justice, *National Crime Survey Report* (Washington, D.C.: Government Printing Office, 1989) Table 6.

105 *Statistical Abstract of the United States, 1982-83* (Washington, D.C., GPO, 1982), 195.

108 Magic Johnson, *My Life* (New York: Random House, 1992), 255.

109 Lasalle D. Leffall, "Health Status of Black Americans," in National Urban League, *The State of Black America, 1990* (New York: National Urban League, 1990), 136-137.

111 For more on Black and White attitudes toward abortion see, *The Gallup Report* (February, 1984, Report No. 281, 17.

114 *Child Support and Alimony—Selected Characteristics of Women: 1985* Statistical Abstract, 1989:368.

119 Quoted in Cade, *The Black Woman,* 66.

119 For a discussion of the punitive regulations of welfare and its economic consequences for poor women see Bergman, *The Economic Emergence of Women*, 239.

Chapter 6 — A Talk With Them

125 "Grandmothers," see E. Franklin Frazier, *The Negro Family in the United States*, (Chicago: University of Chicago Press, 1966), 153.

125 St. Clair Drake and Horace R. Cayton provide a fascinating inside look at the black "Holy Rollers" in *Black Metropolis, Vol. 2* (New York: Harper & Row, 1962), 636-641.

Chapter 7 — Bring Him Back Home

147 Weddington letter to Franklin D. Roosevelt quoted in Gerta Lerner, *Black Women in White America*, 300.

148 Bennett, *The Black Population in the United States, 1989 and 1990*, 9-13.

148 Joy Jones, "Why Are Black Women Scaring Off Their Men"? *The Washington Post*, September 1, 1991, C4.

149 Dorothy Gilliam discusses the plight of Effi Barry in "The Cost of Keeping a Family Together," *Washington Post*, July 5, 1990, C3.

150 Charlotte and Wolf Lesiau, *African Proverbs* (White Plains, N.Y.: Peter Pauper Press, 1985), 23.

Bibliography

Barnes, Annie S., *Black Women: Interpersonal Relationships in Profile: A Sociological Study of Work, Home and the Community* (Bristol, Indiana; Wyndham Hall Press, 1986).

Billingsley, Andrew, *Climbing Jacobs Ladder: The Emerging Legacy of African-American Families* (New York: Simon and Schuster, 1992).

—*Black Families in White America* (Englewood Cliffs, N.J.: Prentice-Hall, 1968).

Boggle, Donald, *Brown Sugar: Eighty Years of America's Black Female Superstars* (New York: Da Capo Press, 1990).

Cade, Toni, *The Black Woman* (New York: Penguin Books, 1970).

Chrisman, Robert A. and Allen, Robert L., *Court of Appeal: The Black Community Speaks Out on the Racial and Sexual Politics of Clarence Thomas and Anita Hill* (New York: Ballantine Books, 1992).

Dalby, Gordon, *Healing the Masculine Soul* (Dallas: Word Publishing Co., 1988).

Davis, Angela, *Women, Culture & Politics* (New York: Random House, 1989).

Duster, Alfreda M., ed., *Crusade for Justice: The Autobiography of Ida B. Wells* (Chicago: University of Chicago Press, 1970).

Faludi, Susan, *Backlash: The Undeclared War Against American Women* (New York: Doubleday, 1991).

Franklin, John Hope, *From Slavery to Freedom* (Chicago: University of Chicago Press, 1969).

Frazier, E. Franklin, *The Negro Family in the United States* (Chicago: University of Chicago Press, 1966).

French, Marilyn, *The War Against Women* (New York: Summit Books, 1992).

Giddings, Paula, *When and Where I Enter: The Impact of Black Women on Race and Sex in America* (New York: William Morrow, 1984).

Glasgow, Douglas G., *The Black Underclass* (New York: Random House, 1981).

Hofken, Nancy J., and Bay, Edna G., *Women in Africa* (Stanford: Stanford University Press, 1976).

Hooks, Bell, *Ain't I A Woman: Black Women and Feminism* (Boston: South End Press, 1981).

Jones, Jacqueline, *Labor of Love, Labor of Sorrow: Black Women, Work, and the Family Life from Slavery to the Present* (New York: Basic Books, 1985).

Ladner, Joyce A., *The Death of White Sociology* (New York: Random House, 1973).

Leab, Daniel J., *From Sambo to Superspade* (Boston: Houghton-Mifflin, 1975).

Leman, Nicholas, *The Promised Land: The Great Black Migration and how it Changed America* (New York: Alfred A. Knopf, 1991).

Lerner, Gerda A., *Black Women in White America* (New York: Random House, 1972).

Malcolm X with Alex Haley, *The Autobiography of Malcolm X* (New York: Grove Press, 1965).

Martin, Joanne M., and Martin, Elmer P., *The Helping Tradition in the Black Family* (Silver Spring, Md.: National Association of Social Workers, 1985).

National Urban League, *The State of Black America, 1990*

(New York: NUL, 1990).

—*The State of Black America, 1991* (New York: NUL, 1991).

—*The State of Black America, 1992* (New York: NUL, 1992).

Pinkney, Alphonso, *The Myth of Black Progress* (New York: Cambridge University Press, 1989).

Pruett, Kyle D., *The Nurturing Father* (New York: Warner Books, 1987).

Scott, Patricia Bell, ed., Double *Stitch: Black Women Write about Mothers & Daughters* (Boston: Beacon Press, 1991).

Simms, Margaret C., and Julianne Malveaux, eds., *Slipping Through the Cracks: The Status of Black Women* (New Brunswick, N.J.: Transaction Books, 1986).

Staples, Robert, ed., *The Black Family* (Belmont, Ca., Wadsworth Publishing Co., 1990).

Williams, Patricia, *The Alchemy of Race and Rights* (Cambridge, Ma.: Harvard University Press, 1991).

Wright, Richard, *Uncle Tom's Children* (New York: Harper & Row, 1965).

MAGAZINES

Barber, Marchelle Renise, "Why Some Men Batter Women: Domestic Violence is America's Most Common Crime," *Ebony*, 45 (October, 1990) 54-57.

Campbell, Bebe Moore, "Black Men and White Women," *Essence*, 22 (August, 1991) 57.

Gite, LLoyd, "Who Earns What?" (African-American Jobs and Salaries) *Black Enterprise*, 21 (August, 1990) 171-175.

Gold, Rachel Benson, "Empty Womb: Black Women's Views on Abortion," *Essence*, 21 (May, 1990) 51-52.

Jarvis, Margaret and Vickie Noles, "Don't Call Me Grandma: Teenage Pregnancy," *Essence*, 23 (May, 1992) 92-98.

Jamison, Charles N. Jr., "So You Want to Be a Corporate Star?" *Essence*, 21 (March, 1991) 65-69.

Jones, Linda, "Do I look Like a Drug Smuggler?" *Glamour*, 90 (February, 1992) 105.

King, Mary C., "Occupational Segregation by Race and Sex," *Monthly Labor Review*, 115 (April, 1992) 30-38.

McMillan, Terry, "Looking for Mr. Right," *Essence*, 20 (February, 1990) 34-35.

Norment, Lynn, "What Black Women Really Want in a Man," *Ebony*, 47 (March, 1992) 30-33.

Randolph, Laua B., "Thinking the Unthinkable: Man-Sharing; A Startling Report From Those Who Do, Don't, Will, Won't," *Ebony*, 46 (January, 1991) 136-139.

Starr, Victoria, "Black Women and AIDS," *Essence*, 22 (April, 1992) 36.

Taylor, Susan L., "Affirming Our Men," *Essence*, 23 (November, 1992) 59.

White, Jack E., "The Stereotypes of Race, (on Sexual Issues)," *Time*, 138 (October, 21, 1991) 66.

Index

LINCC

DATE DUE

GAYLORD · · · PRINTED IN U.S.A.